Practical Ethics for
Effective Treatment of
Autism Spectrum Disorder

Critical Specialties in Treating Autism
and Other Behavioral Challenges

Series Editor
Jonathan Tarbox

Practical Ethics for Effective Treatment of Autism Spectrum Disorder

Matthew T. Brodhead
Department of Counseling, Educational Psychology, and Special Education,
Michigan State University, East Lansing, MI, United States

David J. Cox
Behavioral Health and Technology Research Clinic, University of Florida,
Gainesville, FL, United States

Shawn P. Quigley
Professional Development and Clinical Training, Melmark, Berwyn, PA,
United States

ACADEMIC PRESS

An imprint of Elsevier

Academic Press is an imprint of Elsevier
125 London Wall, London EC2Y 5AS, United Kingdom
525 B Street, Suite 1650, San Diego, CA 92101, United States
50 Hampshire Street, 5th Floor, Cambridge, MA 02139, United States
The Boulevard, Langford Lane, Kidlington, Oxford OX5 1GB, United Kingdom

Notices
Knowledge and best practice in this field are constantly changing. As new research and experience broaden our
understanding, changes in research methods, professional practices, or medical treatment may become
necessary.

Practitioners and researchers must always rely on their own experience and knowledge in evaluating and using
any information, methods, compounds, or experiments described herein. In using such information or methods
they should be mindful of their own safety and the safety of others, including parties for whom they have a
professional responsibility.

To the fullest extent of the law, neither the Publisher nor the authors, contributors, or editors, assume any
liability for any injury and/or damage to persons or property as a matter of products liability, negligence or
otherwise, or from any use or operation of any methods, products, instructions, or ideas contained in the
material herein.

British Library Cataloguing-in-Publication Data
A catalogue record for this book is available from the British Library

Library of Congress Cataloging-in-Publication Data
A catalog record for this book is available from the Library of Congress

ISBN: 978-0-12-814098-7

For Information on all Academic Press publications
visit our website at https://www.elsevier.com/books-and-journals

  **Working together
to grow libraries in
developing countries**

www.elsevier.com • www.bookaid.org

Publisher: Nikki Levy
Acquisition Editor: Emily Ekle
Editorial Project Manager: Barbara Makinster
Production Project Manager: Mohana Natarajan
Cover Designer: Matthew Limbert

Typeset by MPS Limited, Chennai, India

CONTENTS

Matt Brodhead, PhD, BCBA-D, is an assistant professor in the College of Education at Michigan State University. Like many before him, his interests in behavior analysis and autism began at Croyden Avenue School in Kalamazoo, Michigan. Raised in Harbor Springs, Michigan, United States, he has an undying passion for spending time in the great outdoors, especially with his loving wife and adventurous daughter. When he can't get outside, he enjoys listening to and playing music, and in a previous life, he used to tour with a funk band.

David J. Cox, Ph.D., M.S.B., BCBA is a post-doctoral research fellow in the Behavioral Pharmacology Research Unit at Johns Hopkins University School of Medicine, Department of Psychiatry and Behavioral Science. He has worked clinically related to autism and behavior analysis since 2006. His research focuses on furthering a basic understanding of complex choice behavior, the multiple control of verbal behavior, and how those areas of knowledge can be applied to change health behavior and ethical behavior. David can often be found on long runs, hanging with his wife, watching/playing baseball, and sometimes all three simultaneously.

Shawn Quigley, PhD, BCBA-D, is the Senior Director of Clinical Services and Professional Development at Melmark, Pennsylvania. He has supported individuals with developmental disabilities in various capacities over the last 15 years. He has a passion to support the behavior analytic profession through service, research, teaching, and clinical work. In his spare time he can be found enjoying food, sporting events, and the outdoors with his wife and four children.

Series Foreword: Critical Specialties in Treating Autism and Other Behavioral Challenges

PURPOSE

The purpose of this series is to provide treatment manuals that address topics of high importance to practitioners working with individuals with autism spectrum disorders (ASDs) and other behavioral challenges. This series offers targeted books that focus on particular clinical problems that have not been sufficiently covered in recent books and manuals. This series includes books that directly address clinical specialties that are simultaneously high prevalence (i.e., every practitioner faces these problems at some point) and yet are also commonly known to be a major challenge, for which most clinicians do not possess sufficient specialized training. The authors of individual books in this series are top-tier experts in their respective specialties. The books in this series will help solve the problems practitioners face by taking the very best in practical knowledge from the leading experts in each specialty and making it readily available in a consumable, practical format. The overall goal of this series is to provide useful information that clinicians can immediately put into practice. The primary audience for this series is professionals who work in treatment and education for individuals with ASD and other behavioral challenges. These professionals include Board Certified Behavior Analysts (BCBAs), Speech–Language Pathologists (SLPs), Licensed Marriage and Family Therapists (LMFTs), school psychologists, and special education teachers. Although not the primary audience for this series, parents and family members of individuals with ASD will find the practical information contained in this series highly useful.

Series Editor
Jonathan Tarbox, PhD, BCBA-D
FirstSteps for Kids
University of Southern California, Los Angeles, CA, United States

> "An innocent bystander, somehow I got stuck, between a rock and a hard place."
>
> —*Warren Zevon*

You may be reading this book because it is required for a course. Or, perhaps this book has been assigned as part of your supervisory experience. Maybe you are just curious about the topic and you want to learn more about it. You may have opened this book because you have found yourself in an ethical dilemma, stuck between a rock and a hard place, and you are looking for a way to wiggle yourself out. Or, maybe you consider yourself an ethics and behavior analysis nerd (like us), and you are just trying to learn all that you can so you can be better at what you do and what you know. However you got here, we are glad you made it.

Before diving into the content of the book, we find it prudent to first set its context. In behavior analysis, behavior itself is the subject matter, and it is best understood by analyzing the environment in which it does and does not occur. In this book, ethics, behavior analysis, and autism are the subject matter, and you will understand it best by understanding the context in which this book sits.

WHAT THIS BOOK IS

This book is an exercise in expanding dialogue. Although some published literature exists on the topic of ethics and behavior analysis, it is far from exhaustive. This book seeks to add to our understanding of ethics and behavior analysis by highlighting several relevant, reoccurring, and seldom discussed ethical topics behavior analysts face in helping individuals with autism. We hope to expand dialogue about ethics and behavior analysis to these topics. We also hope other behavior analysts recognize and begin expanding dialogue to other topics in ethics and behavior analysis they feel are important and seldom discussed.

We followed a structured approach to expand dialogue to the topics in this book. First, we considered these topics, and potential solutions, in the context of the Behavior Analyst Certification Board's (BACB) *Professional and Ethical Compliance Code for Behavior Analysts* (2014) (hereafter referred to as the BACB Code). Second, and where relevant, we considered these topics in the context of published peer-review literature from behavior analytic journals (e.g., *Journal of Applied Behavior Analysis, Behavior Analysis in Practice*). Where relevant, we considered these topics in the context of published peer-reviewed literature from other healthcare disciplines facing similar problems. Rather than proposing solutions from scratch, we explore how behavior analysts can benefit from the hard work and solutions developed by others. In the end, all analyses, stories, and recommendations are rooted in the BACB Code and peer-reviewed scholarly literature. Though we have included a variety of case studies throughout our book, we enthusiastically recommend Sush and Najdowski's forthcoming workbook of ethical case scenarios for additional examples and instructional resources.

So who might be interested in the topics we discuss? Primarily, it will be people to whom the BACB Code applies. As such, this book is written for Board Certified Behavior Analysts (BCBAs) and Board Certified Assistant Behavior Analysts (BCaBAs), and those pursuing certification. This book is also written for instructors and supervisors of BCBAs and BCaBAs. To keep things simple, we primarily refer to behavior analysts and BCBAs throughout the book. But, know the content and recommendations likely apply to BCaBAs, BCBAs, and BCBA-Doctoral and sometimes Registered Behavior Technicians (RBTs) sprinkled in.

Of final note is the tone of the book. We have read more than our fair share of books over the years. During that time, we have come to appreciate the value of an engaging text. Therefore we have attempted to write this book with you in mind. We have made every effort to write in a way we hope you find engaging, fun, and informative. We consider ourselves to have a decent sense of humor and hope that translates in our writing. If something reads like it might be a bad joke, it probably is.

HOW THIS BOOK IS ORGANIZED

So what are these topics ambiguously referred to throughout the preface? Chapter 1 begins with an overview of the *core ethical principles and paradigms* that form the foundation of the BACB Code. Chapter 1 asks: What are some of the assumptions we make when it comes to ethics and behavior analysis? How might those assumptions help us when we are caught between a rock and a hard place? And, what are some questions we want or need to answer as a field that result from these assumptions?

Chapter 2 is about *contextual factors* that influence the ethical decisions we make. Many different factors have repeatedly shown to influence the choices organisms make—whether they are aware of it or not. Chapter 2 grabs a few of these factors from basic research on choice behavior and research on clinical decision-making and asks: How might these factors apply to ethical behavior?

Chapter 3 continues the exploration from Chapter 2—but at the organizational level. In addition, Chapter 3 flips the script and asks: What can I do about the variables that will impact my ethical behavioral? Many answers likely exist. We offer one in the form of *Behavioral Systems Analysis*. A tried and true behavior analytic approach for accomplishing organizational goals.

Chapter 4 also discusses what we can do as behavior analysts. But, we focus more on the limits of our abilities and the thorny issue of *scope of competence*. Questions asked in Chapter 4 include: What is *scope of competence*? How does the definition of *scope of competence* relate to my own behavior analytic abilities? And, what things am I actually competent to perform?

Chapter 5 starts to look at combining behaviors. Once assumptions are assumed, factors are considered, policies and procedures in place, and limitations identified, we then provide Applied Behavior Analysis (ABA) services. This involves a lot of things. Chapter 5 asks: How can I combine behaviors together to meet my obligations to *evidence-based practice*?

No behavior occurs in a vacuum. Chapter 6 focuses on *interdisciplinary collaboration*. All of us not only have to account for everything discussed to this point in the book. But, we will have to do so while interacting with others who likely have different assumptions, different influencing contextual factors, different policies and procedures to follow, different abilities, and different definitions of what constitutes appropriate practice. Collaborating can be challenging. So, in Chapter 6 we ask: How do I combine my behaviors to interact well with others?

Finally, we conclude with Chapter 7, an analysis of common errors and mistakes that we have observed, with regards to ethics and behavior analysis. We provide these additional points of consideration in order to help prepare you, as much as possible, to avoid the errors of the ways of those who have come before you. Chapter 7 asks: What can I do to ensure my ethical analyses are accurate and complete?

WHAT THIS BOOK IS NOT

There is a lot this book is not. This book is not an analysis of every element of the BACB Code. That book has been written and written well (Bailey & Burch, 2016). This book is also not an official statement or opinion of the BACB. We do not represent the BACB and you should contact them directly if you would like an official opinion on how the BACB Code should be applied in a situation you face (check their Web site for resources first, though). This book also does not constitute any formal advice, whether practical or legal. You should contact your supervisor or a trusted colleague if you are looking for professional advice. You should seek legal council if you are looking for legal advice. Finally, this book is not a primer on ethics, autism, and behavior analysis. We assume the reader has basic background knowledge of all three topics. We recommend you familiarize yourself with these if you have not already done so.

KEY TERMS

Many of the topics and how one might precisely define terms could be book long treatments in themselves. However, we think it is important to define a few terms before we get started. Just to make sure we are all on the same page.

Behavior Analyst. Throughout the book we often use the term behavior analyst. We define a behavior analyst as any individual who: (a) holds a BCaBA or BCBA credential, or a BCBA credential with a doctoral designation; (b) is seeking certification as a BCaBA or BCBA; (c) uses the science of behavior analysis to help a client with socially important behavior change; or (d) uses the science of behavior analysis as their primary approach to researching and understanding a phenomenon of interest. If you consider yourself a behavior analyst but do not fit in one of the above categories, no worries—consider yourself included.

Ethical Behavior. Defining this term has kept a lot of really smart people busy for centuries. We are not looking to pick any fights. But, we need to define this term so we can talk about it practically. We define ethical behavior as "...the emission of behavior in compliance/coordination with the verbally stated rules and behavior-analytic cultural practices guiding practitioner behavior that are espoused by the BACB Code" (Brodhead, Quigley, & Cox, 2018).

We chose this definition because what is defined as ethical and appropriate behavior by one cultural group may be inappropriate and unethical behavior by another cultural group. To avoid these metaethical discussions (and the dozens to hundreds of pages that may be needed to defend our position), we sought to keep things simple and practical. Most behavior analysts work with individuals with autism, are board certified or seeking certification, and are held accountable to the BACB Code. We recognize people may consider behavior that contradicts the BACB Code as more ethical or that there is ethical behavior relevant to their practice that is not covered by the BACB Code. These further support the point of this book—there are a number of areas of behavior analysis where dialogue about ethics and behavior analysis can be expanded.

Ethical Dilemma. Ethical behavior is one thing. But, facing a dilemma can be a whole other ball of wax. We define an ethical dilemma as any situation that meets three criteria. First, the behavior analyst has to make a choice between incompatible behaviors. Second, the behaviors the behavior analyst has to choose from are each supported by the BACB Code. Finally, by engaging in one of the behaviors the behavior analyst violates a different guideline of the code.

We chose this definition because it seems to capture the relevant components of an ethical dilemma. It involves ethical behavior as defined above. It also contains a dilemma—a choice between two good (or bad) options that you cannot wiggle out of and meet all your obligations. If this seems a bit ambiguous, no worries. We provide many examples throughout the book.

MOVING FORWARD

We hope you find this book useful in your practice. Whether you are a professor, trainer, or a BCaBA, BCBA, or RBT working with individuals with autism, we hope our book impacts and transforms you and those around you. And, we hope it leads to greater ethical dialogue on the many important and seldom discussed topics of ethics and behavior analysis.

−Matt, David, and Shawn

ACKNOWLEDGMENTS

MATT'S ACKNOWLEDGMENTS

I would like to thank Jonathan Tarbox for his wisdom and support throughout this project. To Tom Higbee and Dick Malott, thank you for your advising over the years. Thank you to Emma Sipila and Justine Henry for reading and critiquing earlier versions of sections of this book. To David and Shawn, the best coauthors I could ever ask for, thank you for your astute writing and revisions and for hammering away at the final revisions during holiday break (I hope your families will forgive me). To my parents, Thornton and Christine, thanks for letting me grow my hair long. To my brother, Drew, who also grows his hair long from time to time, thanks for getting me, and pushing me to do better. To my grandparents, Mary Lee and Tony Kuchta, who continue to inspire me to live a meaningful and impactful life, I give my upmost love and thanks. And finally, words cannot express my gratitude to my loving wife, Hannah, and my beautiful daughter, Diane; you both give me the strength and courage to overcome any obstacle I face in life, and I dedicate my efforts in this book to you.

DAVID'S ACKNOWLEDGMENTS

First, I would like to thank my wife—Sara Virginia Bollman. She is the definition of support and tolerance. I hope she has not been too worn down by my drifting about the ethical contemplative ocean. Second, I would like to thank everyone at my places of work and within the graduate program at University of Florida. Many of you put up with an endless amount of jabbering related to ethics and behavior analysis. My current understanding of ethical behavior would be severely limited without those conversations.

Thank you.

SHAWN'S ACKNOWLEDGMENTS

I am grateful for the dedication and hard work of my coauthors.

CHAPTER 1

Introduction to ABA, Ethics, and Core Ethical Principles

"Every way of seeing is a way of not seeing."

— Kenneth Burk

What defines the difference between right and wrong; good and evil? Few topics in recorded human history have received as much discussion as what differentiates right from wrong, and good from evil. For thousands of years, humans have killed, imprisoned, sanctioned, and limited access to resources for people who fail to conform to their version of what is right (Harari, 2015). Humans have simultaneously provided various forms of reinforcement (e.g., social attention and material resources) to those who do conform to their version of what is right. These behaviors continue today. The ubiquity of labeling human behavior "right" and "wrong" can be observed through a close look at any group of humans who work together toward a common goal (e.g., members of health professions) or compete for the same resources (e.g., laws regarding theft and market manipulations).

In this chapter, we provide some historical context for different approaches to distinguishing "right" from "wrong" behavior. By the end of the chapter, you should have a better sense of (1) the assumptions that underlie claims of what is "right" conduct for Board Certified Behavior Analysts (BCBAs); (2) theoretical conflicts between different claims to what is "right" conduct for BCBAs; and (3) that applied ethics within Applied Behavior Analysis (ABA) is far from being comprehensive and complete—just like all areas of our science.

The above three points may seem inconsequential to your everyday work as a BCBA. However, this could not be further from the truth. Many BCBAs may not know the philosophical assumptions used to justify the ethical decisions they make. Also, many practitioners may

Practical Ethics for Effective Treatment of Autism Spectrum Disorder. DOI: https://doi.org/10.1016/B978-0-12-814098-7.00001-8

not have realized there often are multiple pathways to what may be called an "ethical decision," and those pathways are guided by different ethical assumptions. Without a working knowledge of these assumptions, it can be easy for BCBAs to misinterpret and/or misapply the Behavior Analyst Certification Board's (BACB) *Professional and Ethical Compliance Code for Behavior Analysts* (hereafter referred to as the BACB Code, 2014).

It is important to describe the historical and philosophical context behind the recommendations that will be provided throughout this book and from which the BACB Code is grounded. From this framework, we can then review practical applications of the BACB Code in autism services. Consider it this way: a behavior analyst is more likely to effectively treat challenging behavior if she understands the context (e.g., environmental variables) in which that behavior was acquired and continues to occur. Likewise, a BCBA is more likely to engage in accurate ethical analysis if she understands the context in which her ethical principles are founded.

PARADIGMS OF CLINICAL ETHICS: PROVIDING THE GROUNDWORK

Behavior analysis as a science and practice emphasizes the importance of consequences in affecting behavior (e.g., Catania, 2013; Skinner, 1938). Although the effects of consequences on behavior have been studied scientifically for over 80 years (e.g., Skinner, 1938), the importance of consequences for "right" behavior has been recognized for thousands of years (e.g., Code of Hammurabi; Hammurabi & Johns, 2008). A quick review of any cultural group will yield rules spanning etiquette, ethics, regulation, and law. In addition to conduct, these rules may explicitly state the relevant consequences (e.g., reward or punishment) for following, or not following the laws (Foucault, 1990).

Rules for conduct and the resulting consequences are not the same for all humans. For example, taking another person's life could result in the death penalty and/or time in prison. However, taking another person's life could also result in positive social recognition. Both outcomes depend on a host of variables such as the dominant cultural group in the geographical location one resides and the context in which the act occurred (e.g., premeditated mass murder vs. enemy soldier in war). Understanding how the application of consequences is justified based on the larger social context is important for understanding claims of "right" and "wrong."

DOMINANT PARADIGMS IN CLINICAL ETHICS

Three paradigms within the realm of clinical ethics are most commonly used to answer *why* different claims to "right" and "wrong" are justified (Jonsen, 1998). They are *virtue ethics*, *consequentialism*, and *deontology*.

Virtue Ethics

Virtue ethics argues that moral excellence, or virtue, is the proper focus or reflection on ethics and rules for behavior (Hursthouse, 1999; Hursthouse & Pettigrove, 2016). That is, certain behaviors are ethical, "right," or "good" in and of themselves—regardless of context or outcomes. For example, honesty and patience are often considered virtuous (i.e., "right" or "good") behaviors regardless of the context and what may happen as a result of being honest and patient. Virtue ethicists label behavior "right" or "wrong" based on what the behavior looks like (i.e., the behavior's formal properties). For example, honesty is considered good behavior because it has the formal properties of a truthful statement. Famous philosophers, such as Lao Tse, Plato, and Aristotle, are credited for popularizing virtue ethics (Marino, 2010).

From this perspective, one may label an individual as virtuous if two conditions are met. First the virtuous individual tends to emit behavior consistent with the socially agreed-upon virtuous label (e.g., honesty and generosity). For example, when documenting and submitting hours spent on billable services to an insurance company, a virtuous BCBA only reports the true type and amount of services provided. Second the individual's virtuous response should be fluent in his or her repertoire (Binder, 1996) and maintained by nonsocial reinforcement. A virtuous individual would reliably behave in a manner labeled as "honest," regardless of any socially mediated consequences that may or may not occur. Given that "virtue" is a social construct, behaviors labeled as virtuous can vary between, and within, different cultures (Skinner, 1957).

Consequentialism

The second dominant paradigm is *consequentialism*. Consequentialism (also known as utilitarianism) argues the outcomes of a behavior determine whether that behavior is right or wrong (Marino, 2010). Consequentialism arose primarily through the work of philosophers Jeremy Bentham, John Stuart Mill, and Henry Sidgwick. These classical consequentialist philosophers argued for what is today called *total hedonistic consequentialism*, which is a combination of *act consequentialism* and *hedonism*. Therefore we describe consequentialism with these two theoretical components in mind.

Act consequentialism argues that a behavior is deemed "right" or "wrong" if and only if that act maximizes the good.[1] For example, whether it is "right" or "wrong" to lie on my tax returns depends on whether I use the money owed in taxes in a way that benefits more people than would have benefitted from the government using my taxes. *Hedonism* claims that pleasure is the only "right," and that pain and aversiveness are the only "wrong." Using a consequentialist paradigm, a behavior is deemed ethically appropriate if and only if the behavior causes "the greatest happiness for the greatest number."[2] Stated differently, we can justify that a behavior is ethical by appealing to what maximizes the good and what minimizes the bad for all relevant parties. For BCBAs, this would be whatever maximizes the overall amount of reinforcers a client contacts in her life relative to the aversive experiences needed to teach her to obtain those reinforcers. Included in the comparison is the amount of reinforcers that would have been contacted without intervention.

Deontology

The final dominant paradigm is *deontology*. Deontology comes from the Greek word for duty, *deon*. Deontologists primarily define what is "good" or "right" as a function of behavior *and* the context in which that behavior occurs. Deontologists establish the central

---

[1] An act maximizes the good only if the total amount of good for all minus the total amount of bad for all is greater than this net amount for any incompatible behavior that the individual could have emitted in that moment of choice.

[2] It should be noted that there are technically many different utilitarian or consequentialist theories, arguments, and considerations (e.g., actual consequentialism; evaluative consequentialism; aggregative consequentialism). However, discussion of each of these nuanced versions of consequentialism is beyond the scope of this chapter. Interested readers are referred to Sinnott-Armstrong (2015).

components of this paradigm by highlighting weaknesses in virtue and consequentialist theories.

Deontologists argue that *virtue theory* is wrong because virtue theory claims specific behaviors are always "right" or "wrong." As a result, virtue theory cannot account for instances where you should not behave virtuously (e.g., lying to your significant other about where you are going to get them to a surprise party organized for them). Deontologists argue that the context in which behavior occurs is also relevant in determining what is "right" and "wrong." Behavior should not be labeled "right" or "wrong" based only on what the behavior looks like (i.e., the behavior's formal properties).

Deontologists argue that consequentialism is wrong for three reasons. First, deontologists believe the consequences of our behaviors are often outside of our control. As a result, consequences are ethically insignificant. For example, it seems unfair to say someone behaved unethically by purchasing coffee that is produced through illegal child labor conditions if they do not know about those labor conditions. Second, deontologists believe that consequentialism places impractical demands on people because you would have to consider all potential consequences for all potential behaviors for all potential people before making a choice (Marino, 2010). Not only would this require a tremendous amount of time and effort, but it also is not clear how all the potential consequences could be included and appropriately compared. Third, deontologists argue that consequentialism fails because it can result in extreme permissiveness. In certain circumstances, consequentialism seems to demand that innocent people be killed, beaten, lied to, or deprived of resources as long as it results in greater benefits for others.

To summarize, deontologists argue that the context within which a behavior occurs has to be considered when determining what is "right" and "wrong." In addition, deontologists argue that the environmental change resulting from a behavior cannot be used to justify a behavior as ethical or unethical. Rather, a behavior is right or wrong based on conformity to a socially derived norm of behavior (Alexander & Moore, 2016).

Deontology can also be critiqued. One critique of deontology relates to who decides the norms of behavior. Often the people who decide these norms are people who have power of some kind (e.g., religious leaders, governmental officials). However, there is no reason to assume those individuals have any greater ability to decide what is right than other members of society. Second, deontology can potentially lead to *posthoc* justification for many different behaviors. If what is considered the correct behavior depends solely on the context, then one could argue the reason they behaved in a certain way was based on contextual factors that others did not observe or consider.

WESTERN CLINICAL CODES OF ETHICS

The above paradigms used to approach ethical dilemmas can influence *how* you justify what is "right" or "wrong." However, these paradigms do not say *what* is right. Therefore formalized codes of ethics, and principles are necessary to guide *what* is right. Similar to the development of ethical paradigms, *what* has come to be considered "right" or "wrong" behavior in healthcare professions has developed over centuries.

Formal Codes of Clinical Ethics

Most modern codes of clinical ethics can be traced back to medicine, one of the oldest clinical helping professions (Edelstein, 1996). Clinical ethics, as it is known today, arguably began in 1803 (Jonsen, 1998) and stems from the Hippocratic Oath that originated between the third and fifth centuries BCE. The early writings of Hippocrates and colleagues focused on the qualities of a good physician and appropriate behavior that physicians should display toward their patients (e.g., gentle, pleasant, discreet, comforting, firm). The writings also included oaths to perform duties required of "good" physicians (e.g., benefit the sick and do them no harm, maintain confidentiality, refrain from monetary and sexual exploitation; Jonsen, 1998). Although what is considered appropriate behavior and duties of good physicians has changed over time, the primary duties from early writings came to be condensed into the Hippocratic Oath and have been adopted by generations of Western medical practitioners.

The first book with *Medical Ethics* in the title was written by Thomas Percival in 1803 (Jonsen, 1998). Percival summarized virtues and duties of physicians with the primary goal of developing rules of conduct that would establish medicine as a profession worthy of public trust. To further formalize these rules, the founders of the American

Medical Association issued a *Code of Medical Ethics* at the Second National Medical Convention in May of 1847. In addition to a formal adoption of Percival's text, the original code forbade advertising medical services to the public, consultation with practitioners using nonevidence supported treatments, and other behavior labeled as dishonest or as occurring without proper education and training (Jonsen, 1998).

Following decades of revisions and name changes, the *Code of Medical Ethics* was published under the title *Principles of Medical Ethics* in 1966. This document had been revised to roughly seven principles. These principles include: (1) respecting the rights of patients, (2) demonstrating ongoing competency and improvement in skills, (3) accepting and respecting the discipline of the profession, (4) obtaining consultation when necessary, (5) maintaining client confidentiality, (6) being a good citizen, and (7) practicing and accepting payment only within one's medical competency (Jonsen, 1998).

Increasing Market Share Through Codification

One of the original goals of establishing an ethical code of conduct for medical practitioners was to demarcate how medical practitioners differed from other healthcare professionals (Jonsen, 1998). Medical practitioners were one of many different professions that claimed to provide healthcare. Medical practitioners sought to create public trust by distinguishing themselves from others who took alternative routes to medical practice. Since this time, medical practice has been remarkably successful in moving from one of many approaches to curing disease and illness to the dominant approach to nearly all areas of healthcare (Farre & Rapley, 2017).

Creating, enforcing, and publicizing that medical practitioners adhered to specific rules of conduct played a role in increasing the size and overall healthcare market share owned by medical practitioners.[3] Many other helping professions subsequently imitated medicine and established their own code of ethics. This allowed them to build public trust and to promote their own services (e.g., practices) to distinguish themselves from other practitioners who offered similar services. In fact, creating enforceable rules of conduct as an approach to

---

[3]It should be noted that it was not just the publication of the rules *per se*. Adhering to these rules likely reduced variability in medical practice between physicians and also improved the quality of the medical services provided. The consequences from following the rules cannot be separated from the rules themselves.

distinguish professions from one another is so widespread that it is now considered an identifiable benchmark in a traditional route to professionalization (Baker, 2005, 2009; Cox, 2013).

PRINCIPLES OF BIOETHICS: THE MATERIAL FOR BUILDING

A variety of historical events led to the modern field called bioethics (Jonsen, 1998). These included advances in medical technologies beyond what traditional medical ethics had encountered, increased interaction between distinct healthcare professions (e.g., physicians and nurses), and increased focus on applied ethics (i.e., ethical dilemmas pertaining to practical everyday life choices; Petersen & Ryberg, 2016). Due to these advancements, there emerged a need to establish basic ethical principles, and an approach to justify those principles, that transcended multiple healthcare professions (Jonsen, Siegler, & Winslade, 2010). The most well-known attempt to establish basic ethical principles and an approach to ethical justification is known as The Belmont Report (Office of the Secretary—OS, 1979).

The Belmont Report

The Belmont Report was written in response to social reactions and problems that arose from the Tuskegee Syphilis Study (Sims, 2010). The Tuskegee Syphilis Study was conducted by the United States Public Health Services from 1932 to 1972. The subjects of that study were 600 men who identified as African American or Black (CDC, 2017). Approximately two-thirds of the men had syphilis and the other one-third did not (CDC, 2017). Importantly, this study was conducted without the consent of the men and under coercive conditions to participate. Furthermore, the men with syphilis were never told they had the disease or that a treatment was available (CDC, 2017). The many disturbing and unethical facets of the Tuskegee Syphilis Study prompted the National Commission for the Protection of Human Subjects of Biomedical and Behavioral Research to establish guidelines for conducting ethical research, which resulted in the Belmont Report. Although originally written to outline standards for ethical research practices, the basic principles outlined in the Belmont Report are also widely regarded as the basic principles of clinical ethics (Veatch, 2016).

The three basic principles described in the Belmont Report are *respect for persons*, *beneficence*, and *justice* (OS, 1979). It is worth noting that the authors of the Belmont Report explicitly indicate that none of the three basic ethical principles are superior to, or carry more weight than, the other principles for influencing clinical decisions.

Respect for Persons

There are two central tenets in the *respect for persons* principle. First, individuals should be treated as independently functioning individuals that have a fundamental right to *autonomy*. That is, each individual (or his or her caregiver) is the most appropriate person to determine what does and does not happen to their body. Clinically, respecting an individual's right to autonomy comes by healthcare practitioners fulfilling their deontological duty to offer choice in treatment alternatives and treatment goals.

The second tenet of *respect for persons* is that people with diminished autonomy are entitled to protection (OS, 1979). Stated differently, "not every human being is capable of self-determination" (OS, 1979). The inability to appropriately determine what happens to one's self may be the result of an accident, "illness, mental disability, or circumstances that severely restrict liberty" (OS, 1979). For example, an individual might request a treatment alternative or treatment goals that place undue burden on someone else—including their future self (e.g., requesting amputation of my limbs because of severe pain that will subside in a few weeks). In these instances the person is entitled to protection from their own harmful decision (e.g., the healthcare team can refuse to amputate their limbs).

Each individual's capacity to make independent health care decisions can be present to varying degrees.[4] Therefore the degree of protection may vary by each individual. Protection comes in the form of a proxy decision maker for those unable to provide consent. Often a parent or legal guardian, the proxy decision maker is assumed to have the individual's best interests in mind and be capable of independently making appropriate health care decisions. That is, individuals with autonomy are assumed to make decisions that maximize his or her benefits gained and minimize harms. Proxy decision makers are

---

[4]A large volume of literature has been written on this from the fields of medical ethics and bioethics. However, these authors have yet to come across a behavior analytic approach to making this decision. As such, it is an area potentially ripe for behavior analytic translation and research.

assumed to fulfill these consequentialist actions for the people they are making decisions for.

Beneficence

The second basic ethical principle is *beneficence* (OS, 1979). The colloquial description of the principle of beneficence, and its companion nonmaleficence (i.e., do no harm), is that healthcare practitioners have an obligation to improve the well-being of others. Fulfilling one's duty to beneficence occurs by engaging in two consequentialist actions.

The first consequentialist action is *primum non nocere*, first, do no harm. This is one of the most fundamental principles in medicine and has guided physicians since the Hippocratic Oath (OS, 1979). The basic premise of this maxim is that healthcare practitioners should avoid harming clients whenever possible. Examples include recommending risky and unproven treatments that have a low likelihood of being successful or conducting an invasive surgery when taking medicine would be equally effective.

Maximizing benefits while minimizing harm is the second consequentialist action. This arose because many health care treatment goals often involve short-term discomfort, but long-term benefits to the individual. For example, individuals with autism that receive ABA intervention within the home environment may have to engage in initially nonpreferred learning activities instead of spending that same time engaging in more preferred free play. However, the nonpreferred nature of these activities is likely offset by the skills gained through ABA therapy and an increase in the individual with autism's ability to access a greater amount of preferred activities and social interactions in the future.

Justice

The final basic ethical principle outlined in the Belmont Report is *justice* (OS, 1979). Relative to healthcare, justice suggests the benefits and costs of health care as a resource should be fairly or justly distributed. No resources are unlimited—including behavior analytic services and the time of the behavior analyst. As a result, practical decisions have to be made as to how the benefits and costs of health care should be fairly distributed.

ABA AND ETHICS: WHAT WE HAVE BUILT SO FAR

Multiple Theories Influence the BACB Code

The current BACB Code has evolved from the ethical paradigms of *virtue theory*, *consequentialism*, and *deontology*. It also utilizes the main guiding principles of *respect for persons*, *beneficence*, and *justice*. In isolation, each of these paradigms and principles can be helpful to guide what behavior is considered "right" and why we think so. However, things become a bit more complicated when different paradigms and principles are combined into a cohesive document.

Influence From Virtue Theory

The BACB Code contains ethical guidelines based on, or justified through, virtue theory. For example, ethical Guideline 1.04 states that: "Behavior analysts are truthful and honest and arrange the environment to promote truthful and honest behavior in others" (BACB, 2014). Here, it is noted that being honest is good. A virtue ethicist may say that a BCBA is truthful and honest because their behaviors are maintained by nonsocially mediated reinforcement. A virtue ethicist may say this BCBA is more virtuous than a BCBA who is truthful and honest only to avoid punishment or to gain social praise. Other examples of virtue-based guidelines include: 1.01—Rely on Scientific Knowledge; 2.13—Accuracy in Billing Reports; and 9.02—Responsible Research.

Influence From Consequentialism

The BACB Code also contains codes justified through consequentialism. Guideline 2.09 states that "[b]ehavior analysts always have the obligation to advocate for and educate the client about scientifically, *most-effective* treatment procedures. Effective treatment procedures have been validated as having *both long-term and short-term benefits* to clients and society" (BACB, 2014—emphasis added). For example, a BCBA would have an obligation to advocate for the use of Functional Communication Training to teach verbal behavior rather than Facilitated Communication. Other examples of consequentialist-based guidelines include: 1.05f—Behavior analysts refrain from conducting services if personal problems interfere with their effectiveness; 2.03—Consultation is required when needed to effectively and appropriately serve clients; and 4.08—Considerations Regarding Punishment Procedures.

Influence From Deontology

Finally the BACB Code also contains guidelines justified by deontology. For example, Guideline 1.05 includes a list of behaviors the BCBA would emit in the context of professional and scientific relationships (BACB, 2014). For example, 1.05a states that BCBAs have a duty to "provide behavior-analytic services only in the context of a defined, professional, or scientific relationship or role." One could easily think of scenarios where positive and negative outcomes arise from strictly fulfilling this duty. For example, it may take several days or weeks to obtain an authorization from an insurance company that allows a behavior analyst to begin assessment and treatment for severe aggression. The time spent refusing to provide service or advice may damage the relationship with a family in desperate need of services, or cause them to seek other nonbehavioral providers that will provide services right away. To avoid this, some BCBAs may choose to start with the client before a funding authorization is in place that defines services to be provided. This can be a slippery slope. The behavior analyst is unable to financially afford to provide free services to all clients in need of services and without current funding. What are the criteria by which some clients get free services and others not? And, how are those criteria justified? Other examples of deontological obligations include: 2.14—duty not to receive gifts or money for referrals; 2.15—duty not to abandon clients; 4.02—duty to involve the client in planning of behavior-change programs; 4.09—duty to recommend the least restrictive procedure likely to be effective.

THE CONSEQUENCES OF INFLUENCE FROM MULTIPLE ETHICAL PARADIGMS

A BCBA's job would be easy if the BACB Code used a single ethical paradigm to guide it. If that were the case, a behavior analyst could determine whether one's behavior is justifiable based on the paradigm espoused by the Code. But, as described earlier, the Code currently invokes all three paradigms to justify different guidelines for ethical behavior. Using multiple paradigms does create flexibility in applying and justifying behavior in compliance with each guideline. However, using multiple ethical paradigms to justify behavior can result in confusion and variability in justified ethical behavior for situations not covered by the Code. Confusion may occur because the theoretical divisions between the three ethical paradigms are assumed by most philosophers to be deep and fundamental (Scheffler, 2011).

Using only one approach (e.g., consequentialism) to justify ethical behavior will directly contradict claims to what is "right" and "wrong" made by other paradigms (e.g., virtue theory and deontology). For example, consider two individuals with autism who are both 13 years old, Casper and Alder. Casper is considered "higher functioning" and needs treatment for social and communication skills. Alder is considered "low functioning" and also needs treatment for social and communication skills, but to a much greater degree. Casper has a much higher likelihood of living his adult life independently and holding down at least a part-time job. Alder has a much higher likelihood of living his adult life in a residential facility.

Between Casper and Alder, Casper is more likely to contribute economically and socially to society. Therefore the consequentialist position suggests that Casper should receive more of a behavior analyst's time and attention. However, fulfilling one's duty to uphold the principle of justice (deontology) suggests the behavior analyst has a duty to provide more time and attention to Alder.

Of greater difficulty are the instances wherein two different guidelines conflict (i.e., an ethical dilemma) and each is justified by different paradigms. For example, consider an ethical dilemma in which a behavior analyst contemplates lying to a caregiver in order to advocate for the most effective treatment procedure. How does the behavior analyst decide between Guideline 1.04 which requires honesty and Guideline 2.09 which requires advocating for the most-effective treatment procedures? Once a decision is made, how does the behavior analyst know if it was the "right" decision? And, how does this decision influence justifications in future ethical dilemmas?

One might argue that whether the behavior analyst should choose Guideline 1.04 or 2.09 will depend on the unique characteristics of the context in which the ethical dilemma has arisen. That is, in one context, honesty should be upheld. But, in another context, the most effective treatment should be pursued and honesty should be withheld. The problem with taking this approach is it could lead to justifying any behavior based on the opinion of the individual. That is, the individual could justify any behavior by claiming the nuances of the context seemed to justify their action (e.g., "I lied, because it is in his best interest not to know the truth"). This could make moot any rationale for having ethical guidelines, like the BACB Code, to begin with.

In summary, all three major paradigms are present to justify ethical behavior within the BACB Code. Generally, each guideline can be argued as justified by a different paradigm. This is not problematic when a single guideline applies to a situation. However, this can limit the generality of the Code to novel ethical dilemmas.

It is unclear which ethical paradigm a behavior analyst should use if they are in a situation that is not covered by the Code. Similarly, it is not clear which guideline should be followed if two different guidelines conflict and are each justified by different ethical paradigms. One solution is to say that different variables in a given situation will lead to one theory being "more right" than the others. However, this seems to result in extreme permissiveness without a formalized manner to resolve this issue.

ABA AND ETHICAL THEORY: WHY BCBAs SHOULD CARE

The history of ethical paradigms and the difficulties they create are important for two reasons. Analyzing ethical behavior is not like fine dinnerware, wherein you only pull out the fine China for a holiday dinner. Ethical analysis is not initiated only on rare occasions when something atypical has occurred. Rather, BCBAs engage daily in behavior that fits within the guidelines espoused by the BACB Code. As a result, ethical analysis also occurs on an ongoing basis and this includes a need to justify why one is doing what they are doing.

Second the field of behavior analysis will benefit by BCBAs understanding how ethical paradigms inform the BACB Code. All BCBAs provide a service under the label of "ABA Therapy." The BACB Code provides guidelines for appropriate behavior when providing that service. If one of the ethical paradigms helps BCBAs engage in more appropriate behavior and provide better services, then more emphasis should be placed on that ethical paradigm. Similarly, if adhering to one ethical paradigm negatively affects service delivery and the quality of services, then less emphasis should be placed on that ethical paradigm to guide the practice of BCBAs. BCBAs can only begin to engage in the conversation of how to improve appropriate service delivery by understanding the underlying ethical paradigms of the guidelines they are asked to follow.

CHAPTER SUMMARY

Theories aimed at justifying why behavior is "right" or "wrong" have been around for centuries. In our current Western ethical context, three dominant ethical paradigms exist. These are *virtue theory*, *consequentialism*, and *deontologicalism*. Each of these paradigms logically conflicts with each other. In a movement toward creating a practical framework for ethical decision making, three ethical principles are often utilized. These include *beneficence*, *respect for persons*, and *justice*. Depending on how these principles are used, different underlying ethical theories may be invoked as justification.

The current *Professional and Ethical Compliance Code for Behavior Analysts* seems to justify various guidelines for conduct using a mix of all three ethical paradigms and using all three ethical principles. This blending of paradigms and principles can create difficulty when BCBAs are confronted with ethical dilemmas. Nevertheless, a composite of multiple ethical theories has been the approach used by most healthcare professions to date. This is likely because each ethical paradigm fails to account for all ethical behavior in all situations. BCBAs should be cognizant of how the BACB Code fits with ethical history and paradigm because it can benefit them individually as well as the field of ABA as a whole.

QUESTIONS TO HELP YOU INCORPORATE
THIS CHAPTER INTO YOUR PRACTICE

1. What cultural frameworks of "right" and "wrong" did you grow up with? How do those influence your interpretation of the BACB Code?
2. Pick any BACB Guideline. Is there a context you would feel justified to violate the guideline? Why do you feel the context justifies that action?
3. Think of an instance you followed a BACB Guideline in the past few days. Why do you think your action was justified? Does your

justification fit more with virtue theory, consequentialism, or deontology?

4. How does adhering to the BACB Code distinguish BCBAs from other "behavioral" providers? How does adhering to the BACB Code distinguish BCBAs from other helping professionals?

5. How do you promote *respect for* autonomy in your current practice? Are there ways you could improve?

6. How do you promote beneficence in your current practice? Are there ways you could improve?

7. How do you promote justice in your current practice? Are there ways you could improve?

8. Have you faced a situation where two different BACB Guidelines suggested conflicting courses of action? How did you resolve the issue? How did you justify your response?

CHAPTER 2

Contextual Factors That Influence Ethical Decision-Making

> "I did not direct my life. I didn't design it. I never made decisions. Things always came up and made them for me."
>
> — *B.F. Skinner*

Ethical *decision-making* is behavior (Newman, Reinecke, & Kurtz, 1996). As such, the ethical decisions you make are a function of the same laws and principles that govern all other behavior. Ethical decision-making involves a *choice context*. A choice context occurs when you have to choose between two or more different responses in a situation. For example, you may observe a coworker lie on his or her monthly report of billable Applied Behavior Analysis (ABA) services. Do you confront them directly, tell your boss, tell the insurance company, or some combination? Or, do you do nothing at all? Analyzing choice contexts serves as a foundation for understanding why humans do the things they do in different situations.

Choice behavior has been studied extensively. In basic behavioral science, researchers have examined the behavioral processes that may affect the likelihood people choose one response over another (e.g., matching law—McDowell, 1989; discounting—Mazur, 1987; effort vs. amount gain—Hursh & Silberberg, 2008). In applied behavioral sciences, researchers have examined the processes and contextual factors that increase the likelihood practitioners and clients choose one treatment option over another (e.g., *Journal of Medical Decision Making*). At the organizational level, researchers have examined how structuring organizational policy around *ethical behavior* can impact business success (e.g., Sethi & Sama, 1998).

Despite the abundance of behavioral research on choice, little attention has been given to variables that influence ethical choice behavior in practicing Board Certified Behavior Analysts (BCBAs). This highlights an important and open area for future research at the basic,

Practical Ethics for Effective Treatment of Autism Spectrum Disorder. DOI: https://doi.org/10.1016/B978-0-12-814098-7.00002-X

applied, and organizational levels. Understanding how different factors affect ethical choice behavior may inform how we train our employees to be ethical behavior analysts, prevent ethical dilemmas from occurring, and improve our ability to appropriately respond to ethical dilemmas when we are faced with one (i.e., an ethical choice context).

In this chapter, we synthesize research in choice and ethics to provide a choice behavior framework for ethical behavior. The chapter is broken into two sections. The first section focuses on basic behavioral processes that have been shown to influence choice and how these processes may influence the ethical decisions of practicing BCBAs. The second section focuses on important topics from the clinical decision-making literature and how those factors may influence ethical decisions made by practicing BCBAs. In turn, using a choice framework will allow you to understand why ethical behavior may or may not occur, and to modify it accordingly. In the next chapter, we discuss variables that influence ethical behavior in organizations. Together the next two chapters provide an analysis of ethical behavior at the basic, individual, and organizational levels.

BASIC RESEARCH ON CHOICE BEHAVIOR

Basic research on choice is often studied in the laboratory. Often, concurrent schedules are used as the context in which choice is examined. At any moment in time, an organism can make one response from two or more concurrently available response options (Catania, 2013). Each response option is typically associated with a different schedule of reinforcement. For example, two different keys may be presented to a pigeon in an operant chamber. Pecking the key on the left results in access to grain on a VI 30s schedule. Pecking the key on the right results in access to grain on a VI 60s schedule. One often used dependent variable in the operant chamber is how many times the pigeon pecks a key each minute. This arrangement therefore allows researchers to examine what variables (e.g., schedules of reinforcement) influence choice between available options (e.g., allocation of pecks to each key).

DIFFERENT REINFORCERS FOR DIFFERENT BEHAVIORS

Different schedules of reinforcement will affect how organisms allocate responding between two available response options. Organisms tend to allocate more behavior to the response option that results in greater amounts of reinforcement. Conversely, organisms tend to allocate less behavior to the response option that results in lesser amounts of reinforcement.

Consider an example of a BCBA with multiple clients on her caseload. That BCBA's time is compensated in the form of money by hours billed to an insurance company. At any point in time, they can spend time analyzing data, updating skill acquisition or behavior reduction programs, or supervising staff—for one client. The amount of time spent working each week is a finite resource and they cannot bill their time (i.e., services) for two different clients at the same time. Therefore a BCBA's allocation of time to the clients on their caseload is a daily decision. The matching law suggests the length of time a behavior analyst spends on each client's case will be influenced by the amount of reinforcement gained from working on each client's case. More specifically, the matching law predicts the ratio of time spent on one client compared to all other clients will equal, or match, the amount of reinforcement gained from working on that client's program compared to the amount of reinforcement gained from working on all other clients' programs (McDowell, 1989).

It is important to note the money that results from hours billed are not the only reinforcers that may affect how a BCBA allocates his or her time. Social interactions occur with the unique set of employees and caregivers associated with each individual with autism. Also, different individuals with autism likely require different amounts of effort based on the skill set of the BCBA and the problems presented by the individual with autism. As a result, the amount of time and effort spent will differ across individuals with autism even though the same amount of money may be earned for each individual (e.g., 2 h of billable indirect time per month).

Allocation of billable time is analogous to responding to different schedules of reinforcement that are present at the same time. For some individuals with autism, only 2 h of work per week and behavior-analytic skills already within a BCBA's repertoire are needed to make the changes to improve a client's programs. These clients require little relative effort. For other clients, the same BCBA may need 3–4 h of work per week (even though they may be able to bill for only 2 h), and they may have to learn new skills (e.g., approaches to implementing preference assessments) or review the research literature to make necessary changes to improve a client's programs. In the former situation the BCBA is on a denser schedule of reinforcement because low effort is put into only 2 h of work. In the latter the BCBA is on a leaner schedule of reinforcement because more effort is put into 3–4 h of work. If each situation represents a different individual with autism on the BCBA's caseload, the matching law predicts the BCBA will spend more time on the first case (i.e., the one with low response effort but pays the same as the one with high response effort). However, arguably, the BCBA should be spending more time on the latter case (i.e., the one needing more work to result in the same quality of programming). Such differences may result in unethical allocation of time and resources to various individuals with autism on one's caseload (see Chapter 1, Introduction to ABA, Ethics, and Core Ethical Principles, for ethical arguments on allocation of scarce resources; see Behavior Analyst Certification Board [BACB], 2014 Section 2.0 for responsibility to clients).[1]

A second example of how different schedules of reinforcement may affect ethical behavior involves client intake. It is hardly a secret that different funding agencies pay different hourly rates for BCBA and Registered Behavior Technician (RBT) services. Basic research on choice behavior suggests organizations will likely accept more individuals with autism from funding sources that pay the best (e.g., the highest) rates. From a business standpoint, this may seem like commonsense practice. However, individuals with autism whose insurance companies reimburse at rates lower than other providers have no less need of services than individuals with autism whose insurance companies reimburse at high funding rates (see Chapter 1, Introduction to ABA, Ethics, and Core Ethical Principles, and principle of *justice*).

As an overly simplified example, Medicaid often pays less per hour of service than private insurance companies (Accelify, 2016). Relatedly, approximately 19% of the current US population is covered by Medicaid, 67% are covered by private insurance, and the remaining

---

[1]Arguably this is one reason why receipt of gifts becomes a slippery slope. Reinforcers are being added to the treatment context that may result in a BCBA spending more time with a client than was agreed upon in a specified contract. However, as noted elsewhere in the book, other contextual factors are also present with gifts that must be considered (e.g., cultural variables associated with a gift exchange—see Witts, Brodhead, Adlington, & Barron, 2018).

14% are covered by other mechanisms or are uninsured (CDC, 2017). If an organization serves clients funded by only Medicaid and private insurance, selecting clients based on a random draw from the population would suggest 78% of their clients would come from private insurance and 22% would come from Medicaid.[2] Research on choice with concurrent ratio schedules indicates people will allocate most-to-all of their responses to the ratio schedule with lower requirements (Bailey & Mazur, 1990; Herrnstein & Loveland, 1975). This would suggest the organization would exclusively accept and serve clients funded by private insurance because they pay more. This would leave clients with Medicaid disproportionately underserved.

The current BACB *Professional and Ethical Compliance Code* (hereafter referred to as the BACB Code) does not directly address the ethics of establishing caseloads based on the reimbursement rates you receive. As a result, BCBAs and organizational leaders can choose clients in whatever manner they prefer. If organizational leaders are unaware of how different schedules of reinforcement impact their behavior, basic behavioral processes suggest intake allocation will lean toward exclusive preference for higher paying clients. It seems difficult to justify failing to provide services to certain clients because their funding rates are lower than other clients with private insurance.

This is a highly simplified analysis. We recognize there is a difference between not-preferring a funding agency because it pays less, and being unable to afford using a funding agency because an organization loses money through the contract as reimbursement rates are too low. We also recognize the amount of work required to submit billable time to some funding agencies is another influential factor (e.g., paperwork, clinical processes). Relatedly, this does not include ongoing changes in reimbursement rates and other variables that influence interactions between organizations and funders. But, see Djulbegovic, Hozo, and Ioannidis (2015) who show how insurance companies and providers can reduce overall cost and maximize profits by approaching healthcare contracts from a game theory framework. Thus the same point of this section holds even when the complexity of everyday settings is considered—understanding basic research on choice behavior is helpful for understanding and modifying ethical decisions.

---

[2]Basic population frequencies: $\frac{\%\text{Insurance}}{(\%\text{Insurance}) + (\%\text{Medicaid})} = \frac{67\%}{(67\% + 19\%)} = \frac{67\%}{86\%} = 77.91\%$ would be insurance.

Understanding how different schedules of reinforcement influence ethical behavior will allow BCBAs and organizational leaders to actively ensure they can ethically justify the choices they make. Continuing the client intake example, it is easy to justify serving a client distribution of 78% private insurance and 22% Medicaid. That is the distribution you would expect when serving all people equally (i.e., just allocation of services to those in need). Deviations from this distribution would mean one group was receiving more services than expected. Organizational leaders could then determine why. Perhaps more of one group seek services from the organization, or the proportion of people from different funding streams differ from national distributions in the areas served by an organization. These would be fair reasons to serve a different distribution of clients because the organization would be serving all people in their area or that seek their services equally. However, if a reason could not be found, it is likely some other basic behavioral process is impacting choice that may not be ethically justifiable.

DELAYED AND PROBABILISTIC OUTCOMES

Not all outcomes in life come immediately after a behavior. In fact, many important and significant outcomes come at some delay. For example the negative health impact of smoking cigarettes may not come for years or decades following any one instance of smoking. As a result, the delayed negative impacts on health often may not play a significant role in the decision of a smoker to smoke each individual cigarette. The relatively small impact of the delayed and negative health consequences on one's decision to smoke is further mitigated by the immediate and reinforcing physiological effects of nicotine. Physical activity provides a second example. The benefits of physical activity do not occur for some delayed period of time. The relatively small impact of the delayed and positive health consequences is further mitigated by the immediate and aversive discomfort resulting from many physical activity routines.

Relatedly, many outcomes in life are uncertain. For example, there is no guarantee you will experience the health impacts from smoking and physical activity. Both depend on how regularly you engage in the behavior, genetic predispositions, and multiple other behaviors that also impact health (e.g., diet). A second example is billing insurance companies for ABA services provided. As many ABA providers can attest, there is no guarantee you will actually get reimbursed for the full number of hours of services you provided to each client. Approximately 200 million medical insurance claims are denied every year for a variety of reasons (e.g., insufficient medical necessity, lack of precertification; Mayer, 2009). There are some things BCBAs can do to increase the probability they will get reimbursed. However, there always is a possibility that BCBAs will not be reimbursed. Reimbursement is an uncertain outcome of providing services.

Basic research on choice has sought to understand how the delay to an outcome, and the probability of it occurring, affects choice. These areas of research are referred to as delay discounting and probability discounting, respectively (see Odum, 2011; McKerchar & Renda, 2012 for reviews). The basic idea behind delay and probability discounting is straightforward. Consider an example where an outcome resulting from a response, or series of responses, is worth $100. People will exert more effort for that outcome, worth $100, if that outcome is delivered immediately. If the outcome is delayed 5 years, or if there is only a 5% they will actually get the $100, they will exert much less effort. The more delayed or uncertain the outcome becomes, the less people are willing to work for it (the less value it has). The more immediate or the more certain the outcome becomes, the more people are willing to work for it (the greater value it has). This pattern of behavior tends to hold for outcomes that could be considered reinforcers and punishers. Below, we provide a few examples of how delay and probability discounting likely play a role in ethical behavior.

Insurance Billing

Consider an example of a BCBA who is responsible for billing insurance companies at the end of each month. That BCBA is likely under at least some sort of administrative pressure to ensure he or she brings in more money than that organization spends (e.g., payroll, facilities overhead, etc.). Due to the inherent variability in clients served and delays to receiving payment from insurance companies, some agencies may be put in a situation where that organization is unable to bring in enough money to cover all costs. The BCBA now has to make an ethical decision and choose whether to engage in behavior that is unethical (e.g., lie about services provided to the insurance company; increase services where two clients are billed at the same time) or that may compromise services and might be unethical (e.g., increase caseload sizes; decrease nonbillable services such as treatment planning or employee supervision).

As one example, lying to an insurance company will result in a short delay to reimbursement, and will result in highly probable access to enough money to cover bills. Lying to an insurance company is also associated with the delayed and uncertain chance of getting caught and contacting the negative consequences of insurance fraud. In contrast, honestly reporting time will result in more immediate consequences which are the highly probable shortage of money and being unable to pay employees or utility companies.

The basic assumption of discounting is that an individual will choose to either lie or honestly report time, depending on what behavior results in the greater overall amount of net gain, or minimized loss, at the moment a choice is made. For example the ABA organization may face a $10,000 fine if caught billing fraudulently. However, if there is no audit mechanism and the probability of getting caught is near 0%, then the amount of that loss is unlikely to influence choice in this context.

Balancing Harm With Intervention Effectiveness
In another example, BCBAs balance the probability of harm from a functional analysis, with the delay to the benefits gained from identifying a more effective intervention. Choosing a descriptive assessment, instead of a functional analysis, may reduce the time to starting an intervention and the serious harm experienced from engaging in the problem behavior. But, this option has to be balanced with the possibility the BCBA may not correctly identify the function through the descriptive assessment. Thus, the time it takes to identify the correct function and implement an effective intervention may be longer than if a functional analysis had been conducted originally.

Whether the BCBA chooses a functional analysis or descriptive assessment likely depends on several variables related to benefits and harms. For example the severity of the problem behavior and ability to modify functional analysis conditions directly impacts the harms experienced through a functional analysis. The total harms experienced are less for disruptive vocal behavior compared to poking one's own eyes. The ability to modify the functional analysis conditions to analyze precursor behaviors or latency to occurrence will also impact the severity of harms experienced by the client (Hanley, 2012).

In these examples the behavior analyst makes a choice between benefits and harms contacted from the descriptive assessment or the functional analysis. Each involves a different delay to the benefits from effective intervention and different amounts of harm from problem behavior during assessment. In addition, each is associated with a different probability an effective intervention will be identified. Each of those outcomes is uncertain (i.e., occurs with some probability). This is an ethical decision because the outcomes of each option directly involves guidelines set forth by the BACB Code (e.g., BACB Guideline 2.09; BACB Section 3.0).

Balancing Time Spent on Program Development

It takes more time and effort to develop programs with greater detail than it does to create programs with less detail. Increasing the detail and nuance of intervention procedures can reduce the probability people will implement the intervention. The more complicated an intervention is, the more work is required for an individual to understand and learn to implement the intervention. Related is the background with behavior analysis for each member of the intervention team (e.g., BCBA vs. parent of newly diagnosed child with autism). The more work required to learn about an intervention and how to implement it, the more motivation will be required to implement the intervention (e.g., Mitchell, 2017). For example, there is a lower probability an intervention will be implemented if it requires a parent of a newly diagnosed child with autism to spend 20 h learning about behavior analysis and 4 h/day of direct observation and data recording—and, they already work 50 h/week and have three other children in the home.

Increasing the detail and nuance of intervention procedures also impacts treatment fidelity. The more complicated an intervention is, the less likely people will be to perfectly implement the intervention (Atreja, Bellam, & Levy, 2005; Muir, Sanders, Wilkinson, & Schmader, 2001). Relatedly, increasing the detail and nuance of intervention procedures increases the delay to when staff and individuals in nontreatment settings are trained with sufficient skill to implement the procedures. For example, consider a differential reinforcement of alternative behavior procedure that reinforces appropriate and varied spontaneous conversation initiation on a FI 60s plus 5s limited hold lag 4 schedule through token delivery and the backup reinforcers include a therapist jumping on a pogo stick while making horse noises. The probability a parent new to ABA understood the previous sentence and will accurately implement the intervention is much lower than an intervention where high-fives and social praise are provided for all conversational statements. Thus, level of procedural detail has to be considered in light of the probability and delay, to high treatment integrity. This is important because treatment integrity has been shown to influence overall treatment effectiveness (i.e., benefits gained from the intervention; e.g., St. Peter Pipkin, Vollmer, & Sloman, 2010).

SUMMARY

Each of the earlier examples highlights how contextual factors explored in basic behavioral research will influence ethical decision-making. We discussed how different schedules or amounts of reinforcement will impact the ethical choices people make. We also discussed how the delay and probability that outcomes occur will impact the ethical choices people make. Being aware of these variables can help BCBAs and organizational leaders implement safeguards so the behavioral processes that occur outside of our awareness do not lead employees to make unethical decisions. In Table 2.1, we have provided

Table 2.1 How to Approach a Clinical Ethical Dilemma	
Step Number	Action
1	Collect *all* relevant data that could help with resolving the matter
2	Identify the basic principles involved and explain how they relate to the case
3	Consider whether principles conflict in this situation OR whether there is uncertainty about what a particular principle (e.g., beneficence, respect for autonomy) directs you to do
4	Formulate a question that reflects the conflict
5	Decide which principles should have priority in this case and support that choice with factors relevant to the case, OR find an alternative that avoids the dilemma
6	When uncertainty persists, note whether there is some missing information that would help you resolve the dilemma. Which information? How will it help resolve the dilemma?
7	Evaluate your decision by asking if it is what a consensus of exemplary BCBAs would agree to do
8	Plan the practical steps that you should take, focusing on the details of the case and the future issues that you foresee
Note: Adapted from Rhodes, R., & Alfandre, D. (2007). A systematic approach to clinical moral reasoning. Clinical Ethics, 2, 66–70. doi:10.1258/147775007781029582.	

a step-by-step process for approaching a clinical ethical dilemma. We hope this table helps to illustrate the specific steps that are likely necessary to engage in a thorough analysis of an ethical dilemma.

FACTORS THAT AFFECT CLINICAL DECISION-MAKING

Every year an estimated 250,000 people die prematurely from medical errors in the United States, making it the third leading cause of premature deaths (Makary & Daniel, 2016). Being a medical patient is as dangerous as bungee jumping or mountain climbing (Leape, 2000)! As a result, a significant amount of research has been conducted to understand medical decision-making processes and how to improve patient safety.

It is unlikely the clinical decisions you make with your clients will result in fatalities. Nevertheless, it is safe to assume that you and all other BCBAs do not make optimal decisions all of the time. By optimal, we mean a decision that will maximize benefits and minimize harms. Below, we describe some important factors that affect decision-making, in order to allow you to further maximize benefits and reduce harm to clients you serve.

LENGTH OF TIME TO MAKE A DECISION

The length of time that a clinician has to make a specific decision will affect the quality of that decision (Thompson, Aitken, Doran, & Dowding, 2013). As the length of time to make a decision increases, so does the likelihood that decision will be optimal. Decreasing the length of time to make a decision will also decrease the likelihood that your decision will be optimal.

Consider an example where an RBT is asked to babysit a client at the home after a therapy session while the parent goes to the grocery store. The RBT may be caught off guard and accept the parent's request if she is asked at the end of a therapy session, has little time to analyze the situation, and was not prepared to be asked that question. However, the RBT would have more time to consider her options, consult organizational policy, her supervising BCBA, and the BACB Code if the parent leaves a message on the RBTs cell phone asking her to watch the child after therapy tomorrow afternoon. In the latter situation, the RBT is more likely to make an optimal decision and politely decline to avoid creating a multiple relationship (see BACB Code 1.06).

The length of time available to decide is also relevant for other ethical decisions. An RBT has to decide within seconds whether to accept a gift presented to them by an individual with autism or their caregiver that they are meeting for the first time. Similarly, an intake coordinator has to decide within a day or two whether or not to take on a new client with severe behavior and low reimbursement rates. A BCBA has to decide within a few weeks or month how to avoid services being interrupted due to employees providing notice they will be leaving. These varied time frames to make a decision will impact the ability of the individual to consider the outcomes of each choice and how each choice option fits with the BACB Code. The more time one has, the more likely one can consider all of their options within the framework of the BACB Code (or ethical rules that may govern their behavior).

AMOUNT OF INFORMATION AVAILABLE

A second contextual factor that influences clinical decision-making is the amount of information available to the person making that decision (Thompson et al., 2013). Generally speaking the more relevant information that is available, the greater the likelihood an optimal decision is made. The less relevant information that is available, the lower the likelihood an optimal decision is made.

Consider a BCBA who needs to choose an intervention to reduce aggressive behavior for an individual with autism. They will likely select the most effective intervention if they have the results of a functional analysis completed last week by a BCBA from a nationally respected severe behavior program. In contrast, they will likely choose a less than optimal intervention if they have no previous information about the individual with autism, were allotted no assessment time, and have to design and write a program to guide RBTs when the client starts tomorrow. Here the amount of information about the aggressive behavior will impact the benefits gained from the intervention and continued harms experienced by the individual with autism and those around the client.

Other examples abound. For instance the type and availability of stimuli that serve as reinforcers for skill acquisition programs will impact the effectiveness of interventions. The more information the BCBA has on what stimuli an individual with autism prefers and is reinforcing, the more effective the intervention will be. As another example, the more information a BCBA has on what motivates cooperation from other service providers, the more effective they will be in getting those other service providers to implement a behavior plan. The amount of information you have for each of these areas will impact the likelihood you design and implement an intervention that maximizes the benefits gained from the intervention and minimizes harms (e.g., BACB Guideline 2.09).

The amount of information you have is ethically relevant beyond Guideline 2.09. Using the examples in the previous paragraph, the information on type and availability of reinforcers aids your obligation to avoid harmful reinforcers in behavior change programs (BACB Guideline 4.10); and information about the cooperativeness of other service providers helps you identify conditions that may interfere with implementation of behavior-change programs (BACB Guideline 4.07). BCBAs are much more likely to engage in ethical behavior if they have more information relative to a clinical decision than if they have less information.

EXPERTISE AND BACKGROUND

A third contextual factor influencing clinical decision-making are limitations on expertise and educational background. Generally speaking the more expertise and background someone has, the greater likelihood the individual will make an optimal decision. The less expertise and background someone has, the lower the likelihood they will make an optimal decision.

Consider a situation where a BCBA has to design a treatment plan for aggression. The aggression has a different function at school (e.g., escape) than it does at home (e.g., attention). In addition, levels of cooperation with the BCBA differ across different teachers at school, and the individual with autism's parents are never available during in-home sessions for training on implementation of the behavior plan. A BCBA with 15 years of experience in the field and who has encountered similar situations in the past will be able to draw on these experiences to get the treatment team members to cooperate and implement the behavior plan to some degree. In addition, they are much more likely to get everyone on board and working together compared to a newly minted BCBA fresh out of grad school that has never had to manage these kind of team dynamics.

Arguably the most difficult ethical decisions are those where two different BACB Code guidelines suggest conflicting behaviors. Whether or not the BCBA quickly identifies the most appropriate action will depend on her expertise and background in how and why each response option is ethically justified. Greater expertise and background with ethical scenarios where the BACB Code suggests conflicting responses and how they subsequently influence the treatment environment will increase the likelihood that the ethical decision made is optimal.

Consider a situation where a parent of a client is choosing between an empirically supported treatment (e.g., Functional Communication Training) and a nonempirically supported treatment (e.g., Facilitated Communication). Of primary concern to the parent is how long it will take for their child to begin communicating with them. The Facilitated Communication therapists told the parent it will be a few weeks before the child will begin communicating with them. The behavior analyst has an ethical obligation to advocate for the more effective treatment procedure (BACB Guideline 2.09). However, they also have an obligation to be truthful and honest (BACB Guideline 1.04). In this instance, does the BCBA lie and mention a timeline similar to or more efficient than the Facilitated Communication approach? Or, does the BCBA remain honest in their timeline in knowing they will lose the client and the child will be exposed to an ineffective treatment? The ability of the BCBA to efficiently make this decision will depend on how often they have faced similar situations and what happened as a result of those previous decisions.

AVAILABILITY OF RESOURCES

A fourth factor that influences clinical decision-making is how easily BCBAs can access the resources they need for effective intervention (Thompson et al., 2013). Generally speaking the more resources one has, and the quicker they can access those resources, the greater the likelihood the individual will make an optimal decision. The less resources one has, and the longer it takes for them to access those resources, the lower the likelihood the individual will make an optimal decision.

Physical things are one type of resource. Consider a BCBA who is implementing the Picture Exchange Communication System with an individual with autism who masters two new novel mands per week (Bondy & Frost, 1994). The ability for the BCBA to have the next set of picture cards ready for the program will be directly impacted by their access to needed electronic pictures (e.g., Boardmaker), paper for printing the pictures, a laminating machine and Velcro, and time to put all of the above together—each of which is associated with some cost. A BCBA has a greater likelihood of having highly impactful new targets available each week if she has access to a lot of resources and can create a number of potential new targets each week. In contrast, there is an increased likelihood the BCBA will pick targets that are used less frequently if resources limit them to only one or two new pictures each week.

Peer-reviewed publications are another type of resource. The pages of the *Journal of Applied Behavior Analysis*, *Behavior Analysis in Practice*, and many other behavior analytic journals provide quick access to resources that aide clinical decision-making. However, peer-reviewed publications that aide ethical decision-making are comparatively scant. BCBAs do have the BACB Code (2014) and books that discuss how the Code should guide behavior (e.g., Bailey & Burch, 2016). But, few resources exist that outline procedures BCBAs can use to make ethical decisions that are not directly covered by the code (e.g., building caseloads in an ethically justified way; distributing resources fairly among clients) or when two different codes suggest conflicting behavior (e.g., earlier example regarding lying to promote the most effective treatment).

Developing peer-reviewed aides for ethical decision-making for BCBAs is an area where future research could have the greatest short-term impact. For example, one set of research questions could revolve around the decisions and resulting outcomes BCBAs make now. BCBAs make daily decisions that impact the benefits gained and reduction of harms experienced by individuals with autism. How well are BCBAs maximizing benefits and minimizing harms currently? How can this be measured? What graduate education experiences improve these decisions? Can those decisions be improved? Relatedly, what would improved decision-making look like? A second set of related research questions could revolve around variability in BCBA's clinical decision-making. That is, where do differences in clinical decision-making currently exist between different BCBAs, and how do these differences impact treatment outcomes? Do the benefits associated with trying to improve judgment and decision-making of BCBAs outweigh the costs?

Summary

Many factors have been identified as influencing the clinical decisions healthcare professionals make—including BCBAs. These factors include things like time to make a decision, information available, expertise and background, and availability of resources. Little research has been published concerning clinical and ethical decision-making of BCBAs. Clinical decision-making directly impacts our ethical obligations to maximize benefits and minimize harms contacted by our clients. In addition, BCBAs face a number of ethical decisions that are not covered explicitly by the BACB Code (2014). Research on any area of clinical and ethical decision-making in behavior analysis could have a large short-term impact on the field of ABA.

CHAPTER SUMMARY

Choice behavior has been studied at the basic level as well as in clinically relevant contexts for decades. This chapter highlights several factors from basic research on choice behavior and clinical decision-making that play a role in the ethical behavior of practicing BCBAs. However, it should be noted that both the basic literature on choice behavior and the applied clinical decision-making literature are significantly greater than can be covered in a single chapter. Hopefully this chapter demonstrated the ubiquitous nature of ethics-related choices made by BCBAs on a daily basis. Relatedly, it is hoped that sufficient examples of ethical decision-making have been provided so readers have a template for approaching ethical decision-making in a systematic manner.

QUESTIONS TO HELP YOU INCORPORATE THIS CHAPTER INTO YOUR PRACTICE

1. Herrnstein famously stated, "All behavior is choice." Identify an instance where you engaged in ethical behavior. What alternative ethical behaviors could you have emitted at that moment of choice? What alternative unethical behaviors could you have emitted at that moment of choice?

2. We identified monetary, tangible, and social reinforcers as likely to vary across clients. What reinforcers did we miss from your practice? How do these influence your current time allocation across clients? How do these influence your current time allocation between clinical and administrative tasks?

3. Can you identify an instance where a long delay to a clinical outcome influenced your decision (e.g., the FA would take too much time!)? Would you have made the same decision if the clinical outcome would have occurred immediately (e.g., FA results in under 5 min)? How long of a delay would be required before you no longer choose that clinical outcome?

4. Can you identify an instance where the likelihood of a successful clinical outcome was so low that you avoided that option? How likely would the option need to be before you would give it a shot?

5. We identified several areas from the basic literature that influence your ethical behavior (i.e., the amount of reinforcers for alternative behaviors, delay discounting, and probability discounting). What are other areas of basic research that influence your clinical and ethical decisions?

6. Think of time where you made a clinical/ethical decision with little-to-no time and you now regret the decision you made. What proactive strategies did you use to prepare you for those decisions in the future?

7. Think of a time where you had little-to-no information to base a clinical decision on. What helped you decide in this context? How do "time to decide" and "amount of information" interact to help/impede clinical decision-making?

8. How does your current ability to access resources impact the clinical programs you design? How do you compete with organizations who have access to more resources?

9. We identified several areas from the clinical decision-making literature that influence your ethical behavior (i.e., time to decide, amount of information, expertise and education, availability of resources). What are other contextual variables that influence your clinical and ethical decisions?

CHAPTER 3

Creating Behavioral Systems to Support Ethical Behavior in Autism Treatment

"Ethics are like toothbrushes — most people use their own."

— *Dave Bingham*

Behavioral services for individuals with *autism* can be delivered in many settings and within many communities. Service settings may include the home, school, private clinic or center, the community, or a combination of the above. In addition, those intervention settings are situated in a range of communities. For example, Board Certified Behavior Analysts (BCBAs) may deliver services: in a large, center-based program on the East Coast of the United States and operate in a major metropolitan city; throughout a major portion of Michigan's rural Upper Peninsula through tele-consultation; within the homes of individuals living on a Native American Reservation in Nevada; in migrant head-start programs with predominantly Spanish-speaking students in Minnesota; and increasingly in a variety of countries and different cultures around the world.

Across all settings and communities, BCBAs share the common goal of improving the lives of individuals they serve through Applied Behavior Analysis (ABA). However, the application of core ethical principles and the Behavior Analyst Certification Board (BACB) Code is likely to be different across different settings and communities. For example, BCBAs in Florida and Detroit are both ethically obligated to minimize the potential for harm and act in the best interest of their clients. To minimize harm, BCBAs providing in-home services in rural Florida may teach kids about natural bodies of water and not to approach alligators. Alligators, of course, do not live anywhere near Detroit. Therefore teaching kids not to approach alligators may be irrelevant and potentially a misuse of instructional time (until it is time

Practical Ethics for Effective Treatment of Autism Spectrum Disorder. DOI: https://doi.org/10.1016/B978-0-12-814098-7.00003-1

for that kid to escape the cold Michigan winter with a Florida vacation). Differences in how core values are applied will differ based on differences in physical context (e.g., the setting and community) as well as social contexts (e.g., cultural differences).

The BACB Code is clear that BCBAs provide effective treatment (BACB Guideline 2.09) and recognize how differences between settings and communities affect how they provide behavioral services (BACB Guideline 1.05c). However, there are little or no published behavior-analytic resources that describe how the unique setting and community will influence the ethical behavior of BCBAs. This is problematic because unethical behavior may result in loss and/or harm to consumers, damage to an organization's reputation, litigation, and/or harm to the field of ABA (Brodhead & Higbee, 2012). Simply knowing and understanding an ethical code does not ensure individuals behave ethically (Cleek & Leonard, 1998; Somers, 2001). If the BACB Code were effective in isolation, unethical behavior would not occur. Ethical behavior, just like any other clinical behavior is a class of behaviors that must be explicitly taught (Newman, Reinecke, & Kurtz, 1996). We would never assume a behavior analyst would understand how to conduct a functional assessment without explicitly training them to do so. Ethical behavior is not different.

Learning to apply the BACB Code can be difficult. The BACB Code must be general in scope because BCBAs work in many different contexts and settings around the world, (e.g., organizational behavior management, behavioral gerontology, autism treatment, substance abuse). Practically, it cannot provide BCBAs with specific details and information to help them with the varied ethical dilemmas they will face. But, therein lies the rub. How can a BCBA ensure they, and their employees, take proactive action to abide by a general code of ethics, while working within their specific settings and communities?

One answer comes from *behavioral systems analysis* (BSA). BSA provides BCBAs with the tools to analyze the environment and create systems (e.g., processes, policies, and organizational supports) that align practitioner behavior with the BACB Code. Within BSA, behavior analysts can operationally define what behavior they expect from their employees and subsequently teach and monitor those behaviors by establishing expectations for employees. Just as supervisors operationally define and measure performance during discrete trial instruction, ethical behavior can be defined and monitored.

In this chapter, we describe BSA and provide examples of how BSA can be applied to promote ethical behavior aligned with the BACB Code. We also highlight how BSA is a flexible approach that allows supervisors to promote ethical behavior unique to the local cultural settings and environments they provide services.

A BRIEF INTRODUCTION TO BEHAVIORAL SYSTEMS ANALYSIS

First, we must define a *system*. Malott and Garcia (1987) define a system as "an organized, integrated, unified set of components, accomplishing a particular set of ultimate goals or objectives" (p. 127). Systems are purposeful. They are not random or haphazard. An example of a purposeful system is a community-based autism center specifically designed to improve social interactions between children with autism and their typically-developing peers. Functional analysis of self-injury (Iwata, Dorsey, Slifer, Bauman, & Richman, 1982/1994) is another example of a purposeful system. Environmental variables are intentionally manipulated with the goal to identify the function (or cause) of self-injurious behavior. Both are examples of systems because they organize components toward a goal or purpose.

A *behavioral system* is a system that involves human behavior (Malott & Garcia, 1987). Examples of behavioral systems include an entire baseball team, a 6-piece funk band, and a friendship or marriage between two people. In the context of ethics, a behavioral system is one in which one or more individuals work to accomplish goals related to ethical behavior. A goal may be as broad as *"The behavior analyst will act in the best interest of the client"* (see BACB Guideline 2.0). Note that "broad" does not mean "vague." A well-designed system includes processes that describe observable behaviors and therefore are measurable (e.g., implements behavioral treatments with a high degree of fidelity). In other cases, a goal may be as specific as *"When collaborating with teachers in a public-school setting, the behavior analyst will respect the values and opinions of interdisciplinary professionals"* (see BACB Guideline 2.03). Again, the system designed for meeting this goal would involve measurable behaviors.

A BSA, then, is the "design, evaluation, and modification of systems to help [organizations] accomplish their objectives" (Malott & Garcia, 1987, p. 133). BSA for ethical behavior is a series of behaviors—a process—that allow organizations to identify deficits (or new expectations) in the ethical behavior of its employees, develop systems intended to meet stated goals or objectives, and analyze outcomes of those systems to continuously improve ethical behavior. As a result, organizational processes informed by BSA are more purposeful and result in better employee performance (e.g., improved ethical behavior).

SIX STEPS OF BEHAVIORAL SYSTEMS ANALYSIS

BSA is a series of behaviors that allow organizations to identify deficits (or new expectations) in behavior of its employees, develop systems intended to meet stated goals or objectives, and analyze outcomes of those systems to continuously improve behavior.

There are many variations of BSA, and most of them follow the same general formula/process (Sigurdsson & McGee, 2015). But for the sake of this chapter, we will briefly describe a process developed by Dick Malott (1974), commonly known as the *Six Steps of BSA* or the *ASDIER process*.

The six steps of BSA are as follows: (1) analyze; (2) specify; (3) design; (4) implement; (5) evaluate; and (6) recycle. The acronym ASDIER (pronounced "as deer") helps for easy memorization of the steps. The six steps are depicted in Fig. 3.1 and occur sequentially.

In BSA, *analyze* refers to evaluation of the natural contingencies. This step helps you understand what variables may be lacking or existing in the environment that may be responsible for a particular behavioral problem. You may consider using the Performance Diagnostic Checklist-Human Services (Carr, Wilder, Majdalany, Mathisen, & Strain, 2013) to assist you with this analysis.

Specify refers to a step in which the behavior analyst describes the performance objectives, the goal(s) to be met. Objectives should be stated as measurable dimensions of behavior and should be described as accomplishments (Malott & Garcia, 1987). As with any behavioral intervention, you should use a precise operational definition of the

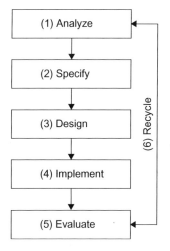

Figure 3.1 The six steps of behavioral systems analysis.

target behavior(s) so you can measure and evaluate the effects of your intervention.

In the third and fourth steps of BSA, the BCBA *designs* an intervention, based on her analysis of the environment and the operationally defined objectives. Then the BCBA *implements* that intervention. Intervention design and implementation can vary considerably across and within behavioral objectives, intervention settings, and so forth. A full outline of these processes would require more space than afforded here. However, the three case studies below serve as examples of the design and implementation of interventions based on BSA.

The fifth step is to *evaluate* the intervention. Evaluation occurs during the time the intervention is being implemented. This step includes evaluation of: intervention fidelity, the measured effects of the intervention on behavior change, and if modification(s) to the intervention would help accomplish the previously stated performance objective(s).

The sixth, and final, step of BSA is to *recycle* until you reach your performance objectives. BSA is a continuous, never-ending, and perpetual process. Colloquially, this process is often referred to as continuous quality improvement. As there is no such thing as a perfect machine, there is no such thing as a perfect behavioral system.

ASDIER, a tool for behavioral enlightenment and systems change.

CASE EXAMPLES OF BEHAVIORAL SYSTEMS ANALYSIS

The BACB Code is broad in scope and may not provide explicit guidance for situations *you*, the employees *you* supervise, and/or *your* organization may encounter. Below, we provide examples of how BSA has been used to help organizations meet specific goals related to ethics. We provide background information to help illustrate the context in which goals were developed and describe the systems that were designed to meet those goals. We also provide examples of how to measure system outcomes.

The examples are provided as a starting point for how you may conduct a BSA in your own organization. Every organization is unique. When reading the examples, you should keep in mind what may be helpful for you and what you may change or do differently. Furthermore, we strongly recommend and encourage you further familiarize yourself with BSA, so you are able to competently develop systems of your own (see Malott, 2003; McGee & Diener, 2010; and Rummler, 2007; for examples).

CASE STUDY 1: A SYSTEM THAT CREATES AN ORGANIZATIONAL CULTURE OF ETHICS[1]

Our first example takes place in a large center-based autism clinic in the Midwest United States. This center provides services to over 50 children with autism and is funded primarily through private insurance. The center employs multiple BCBAs, Board Certified Assistant Behavior Analysts (BCaBAs), and Registered Behavior Technicians (RBTs).

The Problem

The Clinical Director, Lisa, noticed the employees were sometimes engaging in behaviors she felt did not align with the BACB Code. For example, she worried BCBAs were entering multiple relationships with parents of the center's clients (BACB Guideline 1.06); BCaBAs were not basing their clinical decisions on well-supported scientific research (see BACB Guideline 1.01); and RBTs were not documenting important incidents that occurred (e.g., instances when restraint was used or when a client became injured) (see BACB Guideline 2.11). Finally, Lisa observed that BCBAs were reluctant to talk about ethics, as they

[1]The following case study is based on a paper written by Brodhead and Higbee (2012).

associated conversations about ethics as challenging, unwelcoming, and an indication they may face a reprimand from a supervisor.

Lisa knew the behaviors she observed could result in reduced quality of care and consumer protection. Furthermore, she worried that incidents arising from unethical behavior could result in a loss of clients, damage to the reputation of the company, and lawsuits. Finally, she recognized conversations about ethics would likely not be productive if people were not willing to talk about ethics to begin with.

The Solution

After analyzing the problem, Lisa developed the following goals: (1) *The organization will provide ongoing training and supervision of ethical behavior*, and (2) *the organization will create a culture where ethics are openly discussed.* Realizing her goals were broad, she developed and sought assistance to help her achieve stated goals.

Ethics Coordinator

Lisa conceived of a position within the organization that would be designed to oversee the development and implementation of ethics training and supervision. She referred to this position as the Ethics Coordinator. The Ethics Coordinator was intended to be a formalized point of guidance for employees in need of help with difficult ethical issues. The Ethics Coordinator would serve like an ombudsperson that employees seeking advice about potential or ongoing ethical issues could reach out to. The Ethics Coordinator was designed to be a neutral entity that could provide guidance without judgment (to the extent to which the law allows).

Once Lisa decided to establish an Ethics Coordinator, she needed to give someone those job duties. Lisa decided to hire an external candidate, named Melissa. Melissa was not only knowledgeable about ethics, but also had extensive experience in training and supervision.

Individual Training and Supervision

Melissa developed a system to incorporate discussions about ethical behavior into one-on-one weekly supervision meetings. She created a checklist of important topics to cover to provide structure to these meetings (e.g., client treatment progress and parent reported concerns). Discussions about ethical behavior were also added to the checklist, and supervisors were trained to use the checklist.

Melissa trained the supervisors to discuss common ethical dilemmas and situations their supervisees may experience. There are no published studies that show how to teach ethical behavior in ABA. Therefore Melissa extrapolated that vocal reports and role play may be one efficient route to teach ethical behavior. For example, the supervisors were trained to discuss ethical situations they had personally encountered and how they responded appropriately to each situation.

Melissa also trained the supervisors to engage their supervisees in dialogue about potential ethical situations. This dialogue provided supervisors with the opportunity to give feedback on whether they had encountered an ethical problem, based on the verbal report of the supervisee. If the supervisee did encounter an ethical problem, their verbal report also provided an opportunity for feedback on the actions taken.

Finally, Melissa asked the supervisors to continuously archive ethical situations encountered by employees who worked for the organization. The organization quickly developed a long list of examples that could be used for discussion in weekly supervision meetings. These examples also served as excellent training materials for new employees. The archive turned out to be of great value to the organization because the organization had ethics content for training that was *relevant* and *meaningful* to that specific organization.

Group Training and Supervision

Melissa also developed a group training and supervision model. She scheduled annual trainings related to topics of ethical behavior that were frequently encountered within the organization (e.g., entering multiple relationships with client parents). Melissa provided examples and nonexamples of potential ethical dilemmas which provided employees with an opportunity to respond and receive feedback. At the end of each training, she provided an opportunity for additional questions related to ethics.

Process Map

The role of the Ethics Coordinator is further depicted in Fig. 3.2. The Ethics Coordinator supervises the implementation of individual

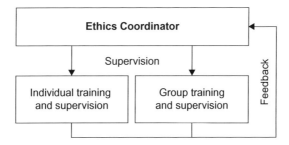

Figure 3.2 A process map depicting the role of the Ethics Coordinator.

training and supervision, and group training and supervision. Outcomes are produced from both individual and group training and supervision components, and these outcomes serve as feedback for the Ethics Coordinator, who uses that feedback to make future improvements.

Measuring Outcomes and Conclusion

Lisa took special care to observe the behaviors that originally concerned her: entering multiple relationships, lack of scientific decision-making, and poor incident documentation. In areas she did not see improvement, she worked closely with Melissa to improve system outcomes and routinely monitored those outcomes. Lisa developed measures to assess the quality of trainings created and provided by Melissa. She also asked Melissa to track the number of questions she received from organizational employees. Lisa routinely observed one-on-one supervision meetings, and she kept track of the number of archived ethical scenarios.

The above case study serves as an example of BSA applied to ethical behavior. Lisa recognized she wanted ethical behavior to improve at her organization. This led to an analysis of environmental factors that aided in the design, implementation, and evaluation of multiple components organized into a cohesive system. This system was designed to meet the specific goals of *providing ongoing training and supervision of ethical behavior,* and *creating a culture where ethics are openly discussed.*

CASE STUDY 2: A STEP-BY-STEP PROCESS FOR INTERACTING WITH NONBEHAVIORAL PROFESSIONALS[2]

Our next example takes place in the intermountain Western United States. Jared was a Board Certified Behavior Analyst-Doctoral with a PhD in Special Education and ran a small consultation firm. Most of his contracts were with public schools where he and his associates helped public schools build capacity to serve individuals with autism. He employed two BCBAs who grew up in the area and completed their master's degree programs at a local university.

The Problem

One afternoon, Jared sent one of his BCBAs (Nate) to attend an Individualized Education Program (IEP) planning meeting. This meeting was for a student who attended a district Jared had established a contract with. Also at the meeting, on behalf of the school district, was a Speech–Language Pathologist (SLP), an Occupational Therapist (OT), the special education teacher, and the Director of Special Education. The student's father was also in attendance.

The SLP began a discussion about her recommendations to improve the student's language outcomes because the student had major deficits in language. To Nate, her recommendations sounded odd and misguided because the recommendations appealed to hypothetical constructs, such as cognition. Nate was also concerned because the SLP did not mention any verbal behavior interventions he was familiar with and felt were the best approach to teaching language (e.g., Barbera, 2007).

Nate began to question the professional judgment of the SLP. He asked her to explain the research supporting her recommendations and insisted she familiarize herself with the verbal behavior approach. The OT and special education teacher sat in disbelief of Nate's combative behavior and the Director of Special Education sat back in disgust. The parent expressed he was extremely confused and, from that point forward, there was minimal trust between Nate, the school, and the parent. Following the meeting, the Director of Special Education called Jared to report Nate's unprofessional behavior. The Director of Special Education expressed that respect for Nate had been lost and

---

[2]The following case study is based on a paper written by Brodhead (2015).

she would terminate the district's contract with Jared's firm if this happened again.

Jared was rightfully frustrated with Nate's behavior at the IEP meeting. However, Jared understood that Nate was not to blame. Instead, Jared knew *the organism is always right*. Jared had not done enough to arrange the environment so his employees learned how to effectively cooperate with professionals from other disciplines (BACB Guideline 2.03) while acting in the best interest of their clients (BACB Guideline 2.0) and maintaining high professional standards (BACB Guideline 1.0).

The Solution
To prevent uncooperative behavior from happening again (for Nate and other associates), Jared developed the following goal: *The BCBA will respect the values and opinions of interdisciplinary professionals*. This goal led to the development of a task analysis designed to guide employees through a series of questions that should be considered before responding to a nonbehavioral treatment recommendation presented by a colleague.

Task Analysis
The task analysis Jared created included the following items to be considered: (a) will the proposed treatment physically harm the client; (b) what research supports the proposed treatment; (c) can the treatment be translated into behavioral principles; (d) how much will the treatment negatively affect the outcomes of the client; (e) what is the likelihood the treatment will negatively affect the outcomes of the client? Following consideration of the above items, the final step in the task analysis had the BCBA answer the questions, "Given what I have learned, does it really benefit the client for me to question the judgment of my colleague?" See Fig. 3.3 for a visual depiction of this analysis.

Following the development of the task analysis, Jared presented it to his BCBAs along with multiple case examples of nonbehavioral treatment recommendations. Jared provided feedback to his BCBAs as they discussed their process of decision-making. Jared also modeled appropriate ways to discuss nonbehavioral treatments with colleagues. Jared then provided his BCBAs with opportunities to independently

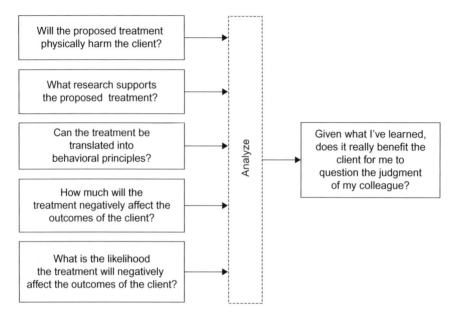

Figure 3.3 A visual depiction of the analysis developed by Jared. Each question is answered, and all answers are analyzed to provide context and consideration for the final question of whether or not questioning the nonbehavioral treatment is beneficial.

complete the checklist and formulate a decision of whether to address the nonbehavioral treatment. If necessary, BCBAs also role-played appropriate ways to discuss alternatives to nonbehavioral treatments.

Measuring Outcomes and Conclusion

Jared measured the accuracy of responding to each component of the checklist for each BCBA. Knowing his observations did not capture performance in the natural environment, Jared developed social-validity surveys and e-mailed them to colleagues that interacted with the BCBAs he employed (see Luiselli, 2015). Jared used the returned surveys to provide feedback to further improve the professional interactions of his BCBAs.

This case study describes an analysis of the environment that led to the design, implementation, and evaluation of a system aimed at accomplishing the specific goal of: *BCBAs respecting the values and opinions of interdisciplinary professionals.* By spending some time operationalizing expectations for interdisciplinary collaboration, Jared could describe observable and measurable behaviors his BCBAs could engage in. After providing feedback during training sessions and soliciting additional feedback from colleagues through social-validity surveys, Jared successfully used BSA to help meet his goal.

CASE STUDY 3: ENSURING CLIENT AND CAREGIVER CONSENT IN TREATMENT

Our final example takes place in the West Coast of the United States. Patty was a BCBA who worked for a small agency contracted by the state to provide in-home services to low-income families. Due to budget constraints, Patty could visit each home only once a month for a few hours. Patty had to make the most of her time during her visits.

The Problem

One morning, Patty entered a home of an immigrant family and found a mother and multiple children in the house. The mother spoke English as a second language but articulated the children belonged to her brothers, sisters, and family friends. She collectively referred to the children as cousins. The mother was not familiar with the Western model of mental-health services. The mother introduced her daughter, Celia, and Patty watched as Celia played with her cousins. Patty quickly observed Celia behaving aggressively toward her cousins as well as that Celia could not talk and understood very few basic commands. Patty decided the first goal for her behavior change program would be to decrease Celia's hitting behavior.

Patty conducted a brief functional assessment and felt confident Celia's aggressive behavior occurred because it resulted in access to her cousins' attention. Patty then conducted functional communication training trials where she taught Celia to give a small, white laminated card that said "Play with me!" to one of her cousins in exchange for their attention. Celia quickly learned to give the card to her cousins and her hitting behavior decreased. Before leaving, Patty spoke with Celia's mom and told her what she had done. Celia's mom nodded as Patty spoke but Patty was not sure if Celia's mom understood. However, Patty was not too concerned because the cousins seemed to understand what to do and Celia had quickly learned to gain their attention without hitting them. Patty's job was hard, and she was not used to having so much success in such little time. She was proud of what she had accomplished.

A few weeks later Patty was called by her supervisor, Kate. An immigration advocate working for Celia's family had called the agency and threatened to file a formal complaint with the state. The advocate's first concern was that Celia's mom was upset Patty had taught Celia to communicate with a white laminated card. Celia's mom did not understand the point of the card and found it demeaning. Celia's mom was also upset because the hitting behavior that Patty had identified as inappropriate was a *culturally appropriate way of gaining attention.*

The advocate's second concern was that Patty had not obtained consent and consulted with Celia's mom prior to behavioral assessment and treatment. When the advocate asked Celia's mom if Patty had asked her if the behavior change program was acceptable, Celia's mom said no, but had not considered questioning Patty because she was unfamiliar with Western health care and the requirement to obtain consent before treatment. To summarize, Patty did not obtain consent for assessment and treatment (BACB Guideline 3.03) and she failed to understand how differences in culture affect service delivery (BACB Guideline 1.05c).

The Solution
Kate (Patty's supervisor) was determined to avoid future similar situations. Besides Patty's potential violations of BACB Guidelines 1.05c and 3.03, Kate feared any formal complaints may result in the loss of future contracts with the state. Therefore Kate developed systems to help meet the following goals: (1) *BCBAs will always obtain client consent prior to assessment and treatment* and (2) *BCBAs will always choose culturally appropriate assessments and interventions.*

Obtaining Consent
Kate developed a brief consent form for families to sign before BCBAs could conduct assessment and treatment. This consent form outlined what services would be provided, why they would be provided, and what could be expected from the family. The consent form also described the rights of the family (e.g., the right to refuse treatment and have input in treatment planning) and provided contact information to a nonprofit mental health advocacy agency to whom families could bring questions.

The design and implementation of a consent form may sound silly. Perhaps, because it seems like a no-brainer. Is not obtaining consent *prior* to assessment and treatment considered ABA 101? But, sometimes we forget the most obvious duties when our passion for other aspects of ABA are at strength. BACB Guideline 2.09a states that "[c] lients have a right to effective treatment." As applied behavior analysts, our underlying values as a helping profession may lead to us treat a behavioral problem without obtaining explicit consent. When a caregiver of a new client invites a BCBA to their home, consent may seem implied to assess and treat behavioral excesses and deficits based on our understanding of the most effective way to do so. As an analogy, an emergency room doctor in the United States would feel justified to prevent a patient from bleeding out—even if the patient does not speak English and is unable to consent to physically invasive treatments. By presenting themselves in the emergency room, implied consent exists for the doctor to effectively treat the patient's problem.

But implied consent does not equate to explicit consent. BCBAs in Patty's situation may therefore experience an ethical dilemma with two guidelines in conflict with one another (i.e., act in the best interest of the client by treating them now, or obtain consent then treat them later). As you may remember from Chapter 2, Contextual Factors that Influence Ethical Decision-Making, the time constraints to make a decision and delays to the outcomes of our decisions can affect our judgment. In Patty's case, her passion for treatment plus the need to decide in that moment likely caused her to make the inappropriate decision to treat a behavior without explicit consent. Had Celia's problem behavior been more severe and potentially life-threatening, the decision to treat *without consent* would likely be justified.

Kate also worked with the immigration advocate to develop variations of the consent form that would be more culturally appropriate to families from different cultural backgrounds. Doing so allowed Kate to identify differences between cultures more easily. In turn, this allowed the agency to better infer what clients from different cultural backgrounds may value, and better predict and prepare for the needs those clients may have. The immigration advocate noted this was better than assuming client cultural values were not important. The agency then partnered with a nonprofit organization that provides interpreters for situations where clients do not speak English as a first language.

Culturally Appropriate Assessment and Intervention

Though you may think that Patty should have known to obtain consent *prior* to assessment and treatment, do not forget that the *organism is always right*. In this case, something was missing from the environment that resulted in this procedural oversight. The fact she did not recognize how her own values may have differed from those of her clients is much more complicated and nuanced. This is because very little has been written from a behavioral perspective that evaluates the effect of culture on choosing intervention goals, designing culturally appropriate interventions, or how cultural background influences behavioral intervention outcomes (Brodhead, Durán, & Bloom, 2014; Fong, Catagnus, Brodhead, Quigley, & Field, 2016).

In addition to the steps mentioned earlier, Kate also implemented several procedures to increase the likelihood of implementing culturally appropriate assessments and interventions in the future. First, she made efforts to hire BCBAs from diverse cultural backgrounds to increase the chances her agency could be culturally responsive. Second, she arranged for BCBAs at her agency to meet with leaders from various cultural groups (e.g., ministers and community activists). Meeting these leaders allowed the BCBAs to better understand the values of those groups and helped the BCBAs recognize their own biases and how those biases affect their clinical decisions. For example, one BCBA recognized how his indifference towards organized religion affected his ability to adequately assist clients who required support in religious settings.

Measuring Outcomes and Conclusion

Kate's newly developed consent process ensured that consent forms were provided and signed by all clients or their caregivers prior to BCBAs conducting behavioral assessments and treatment. Kate measured the number of variations on behavior plans that were designed for specific cultural groups. Finally, Kate measured the number of culturally diverse employees in her agency. As a result of Kate's efforts, community leaders were grateful that her agency was showing initiative and sensitivity to their unique and important needs.

The above case study highlights an important point. Organizations need to be accommodating to the various cultures they serve. BSA allowed this organization to develop a systematic way to accomplish goals surrounding cultural awareness based on the unique individuals they work with. More specifically, a BSA proved helpful to assist Kate meet her goals of *obtaining client consent prior to assessment and treatment*, and *choosing culturally appropriate behaviors for assessment and intervention*.

CHAPTER SUMMARY

Ethical behavior can be specific to the setting and community where services are delivered. Individuals implementing ABA may be confronted with regular ethical decisions specific to those settings and communities. BSA is one approach that can help organizational leaders establish goals, design systems to observe and measure ethical behavior, and create organizational supports to foster ethical behavior specific to their agency. In this chapter, we provided three case studies to show how BSA may be used toward this end. Though every organization is unique, we hope these examples provide you with a framework with which you may conduct your own BSA for your own organization.

QUESTIONS TO HELP YOU INCORPORATE THIS CHAPTER INTO YOUR PRACTICE

1. What are three examples for how the generality of the BACB Code is difficult to translate to the specifics of your clinical practice?
2. What systems do you currently have at your organization to improve the clinical behaviors of those you supervise (e.g., quality assurance, regular supervision meetings)? What systems do you currently have at your organization to improve the *ethical* behavior of those you supervise?
3. Answer the questions from 2—but for your own behavior. Is there a difference in amount, degree, effort, etc., of the monitoring systems for those you supervise compared to monitoring systems for you?
4. How do the systems identified in questions 2 and 3 fit within the BSA framework? What components are you missing? What additional components do you have?
5. What would be the benefits and drawbacks to having an identified Ethics Coordinator in your organization? Would an Ethics

Committee increase or decrease those benefits and drawbacks? What would be the benefits and drawbacks to having no formalized Ethics Coordinator or Ethics Committee at your organization?

6. We identified collaboration with colleagues from other professions and upholding ongoing treatment consent as common examples that benefitted from a BSA approach. What are three clinical areas of your current organization that could benefit from BSA? What are three *ethical* areas of your current organization that could benefit from BSA?

CHAPTER 4

Identifying Your Scope of Competence in Autism Treatment

"They say 'stay in your lane boy, lane boy.'"

—*Tyler Joseph*

We begin this chapter with a story.

Jack was a Board Certified Behavior Analyst (BCBA) and clinical director of a center-based program for individuals with autism. He was in charge of over-seeing the behavioral therapy of 15 clients who attended the program for 30—40 hours per week. Though Jack had been a BCBA for only 4 years, he had worked for the center-based program for 8 years, and rose through the ranks to obtain his current position. During his graduate coursework, a heavy emphasis was placed on behavioral principles related to skill acquisition (e.g., language and social-skill development). In addition, Jack received his BCBA practicum supervision from someone widely regarded as an expert in verbal behavior. Overall, Jack was doing well with his center-based programs.

One day, Jack received a referral for Theo, an 18-year-old male with severe autism. Theo was reported to display severely aggressive behavior towards his parents and teachers. However, Jack did not observe any aggressive behavior when he met Theo. Theo also was reported to exhibit very little functional language, which Jack corroborated during Theo's intake assessment.

Jack felt he could help Theo by teaching him how to talk and socialize as Jack had done with many of his clients in the past. As a result, Jack believed Theo's aggressive behavior would go away. Jack also believed Theo's aggression must not be all that bad, as he had not observed it when he met Theo. With that, Jack accepted Theo into his center.

Theo began engaging in aggressive behavior immediately upon starting at Jack's center. Theo frequently threw chairs in anger, and he often pulled hair out of the heads of the employees he was working with. When asked to complete simple academic tasks, Theo would run away into an adjacent room. It became a never-ending battle to track Theo down, contain him, and bring him back to his behavioral therapy room.

One day, employees at Jack's center were looking for Theo, who had recently ran away from large-group instruction. An employee eventually found Theo in the corner of a dark room, and immediately noticed that Theo was

Practical Ethics for Effective Treatment of Autism Spectrum Disorder. DOI: https://doi.org/10.1016/B978-0-12-814098-7.00004-3

masturbating. The employee told Theo to stop, and Theo immediately punched the employee so hard that the employee suffered a mild concussion.

Eventually, Theo was running away from employees to hide and masturbate up to 15 times per day. Every time an employee tried to interrupt or stop Theo, he became extremely aggressive. Jack tried everything to get Theo's aggression and sexual behavior under control. He tried functional communication training (e.g., Tiger, Hanley, & Bruzek, 2008), he tried differential reinforcement of other behavior (e.g., Jessel & Ingvarsson, 2016), and he tried to provide choices between activities (e.g., Dunlap et al., 1994). Nothing worked to reduce Theo's challenging behaviors, even with a functional analysis as context to inform treatment. Jack was stuck, and meanwhile, eight months went by and Theo made very little progress.

The story of Jack and Theo may sound like an academic fairytale that professors make up to scare graduate students. However, the story of Jack and Theo is true, and we have experienced or heard many stories with the same plotline: a BCBA accepts a case he is not qualified to treat, and problems ensue for the client, Registered Behavior Technicians (RBTs), and the BCBA.

Why does this happen? Treatments based upon the science of behavior analysis have widely improved the human condition. In addition to a robust evidence-base for the treatment of autism, the power of behavior analysis has been demonstrated in applications across a variety of other populations and settings. Some of these populations, settings, and problems include geriatrics (e.g., Baker & LeBlanc, 2015), organizations (Bucklin, Alvero, Dickinson, Austin, & Jackson, 2000), workplace safety (Hyten & Ludwig, 2017), substance abuse and misuse (e.g., Jarvis & Dallery, 2017), writer's block (e.g., Didden, Sigafoos, O'Reilly, Lancioni, & Sturmey, 2007; Molloy, 1983; Upper, 1974), and landmine detection (La Londe et al., 2015). These robust findings support the widely held conviction amongst BCBAs that *the principles of behavior are universally applicable.*

But, as President Harry Truman once said, "*With great power goes great responsibility.*" We may be tempted to see and use behavior analysis as a cure for all the world's ills we may face. However, each BCBA has a responsibility to only use behavior analysis in the area or areas in which she is competent. Failing to practice only within one's area of competence can have several negative outcomes.

One negative outcome is a waste of treatment time and resources. Every client, employee, and agency have limits to the number of hours they are able to be in a therapeutic setting. Relatedly, every employee and agency has a limit to the resources they can spend to help clients and RBTs maximize treatment outcomes through the time spent in therapy. In the example provided earlier, Theo's time was being wasted as a more qualified BCBA could have had better outcomes had Jack been honest with his abilities. Similarly, Jack and the RBTs' time were being wasted as they could have used that time with a client they were competent to serve. The Behavior Analyst Certification Board (BACB) Code obligates BCBAs to identify conditions that interfere with implementation of effective behavior-change programs (BACB, 2014— Guideline 4.07). Sometimes, the current supervising BCBA is the interfering condition.

A second negative outcome is misuse or misapplication of behavior analysis. Practicing outside of one's competence increases the likelihood one will fail to take into account relevant disorder- and setting-specific variables important to treatment design. Put another way, "*You don't know what you don't know.*" This could result in misusing and misapplying behavior analysis in the design and implementation of an intervention. For example, Jack may not be familiar or competent with relevant clinical procedures for assessing and designing programs around sexual behaviors (e.g., Reyes, et al., 2011, 2017; Walker et al., 2014). In turn, the necessary safeguards and training for the client and RBTs are likely to be missing, and the effectiveness of the assessments and intervention program reduced.

A third negative outcome may be an impacted ability to continue to practice as a BCBA. The BACB Code has outlined that BCBAs only practice "within the boundaries of their competence, defined as being commensurate with their education, training, and supervised experience" (1.02, p. 4). Practicing outside of one's competence directly violates the BACB Code. As of 2016, BCBAs are required to comply with the BACB Code and violation may result in loss of certification (BACB, 2014).

But exactly how do we know what our scope of competence is? How does scope of competence differ from scope of practice? And, how does the BACB Code define a BCBA's scope of competence in behavior analysis? In the following section, we answer these questions and integrate case studies to illustrate the nuances required to adhere to this very important BACB Code.

SCOPE OF COMPETENCE WITHIN SCOPE OF PRACTICE[1]

To understand *scope of competence*, one has to first understand *scope of practice*. People often confuse these terms, but they are very different. *Scope of practice* can be defined as "the range of activities in which members of a profession may be authorized to engage by virtue of holding a credential or license." This "range of activities" may be defined by a credentialing or certifying agency (e.g., the BACB Task List, 2012). Or, this "range of activities" may be defined legally through state laws and licensing requirements (e.g., behavior analyst licensure boards in the state of New York). Sometimes, a licensure law will conflict with the scope of practice outlined by the BACB credential. For example, a behavior analyst's scope of practice may be more narrowly defined by a state licensure law compared to the BACB Task List. When this happens, the licensure law "trumps" the scope of practice guidelines of the BACB.

Defining *scope of practice* allows identification of qualified and unqualified professionals. Identifying qualified and unqualified individuals is important for funders (e.g., private insurance companies) and consumers of the services (Green & Johnston, 2009). Consider the example of Theo and aggressive behavior. An insurance company and Theo's parents would likely seek out treatment provided by Jack because functional assessment and treatment of problem behavior are within the *scope of practice* outlined by Jack's BCBA credential. However, things would be different if Theo had difficulty with motor behavior related to articulation (i.e., correct movement of mouth musculature to enunciate sounds correctly). Here, an insurance company and Theo's parents would likely seek out treatment by a Speech–Language Pathologist (SLP) because of the skills an SLP has through their specific credential (i.e., Certificate of Clinical Competence for Speech–Language Pathologist (CCC-SLP)). Though both credentials are relevant to helping individuals with autism, each credential delineates the specific knowledge, skills, and abilities between the different professionals.

Scope of competence differs from *scope of practice*. Where *scope of practice* was defined at the level of a profession, *scope of competence* is

---

[1]The following sections are based loosely on a forthcoming paper by Brodhead, Quigley, & Wilczynski.

defined at the level of the individual practicing within a profession. Specifically, *scope of competence* refers to the "the range of professional activities of the individual practitioner that are performed at a level that is deemed proficient." Though a BCBA's scope of practice is described by the BACB or a licensing agency, his or her scope of competence is determined by each BCBA's unique experiences and training as a professional.

Let us return to the example of Jack and Theo. Functional assessment and treatment of severe aggression is described as within the scope of practice for Jack because he holds a BCBA credential. However, his *scope of competence* is in designing programs to teach language and social skills. Jack's competence is determined, in part, by his graduate coursework, the setting and his experiences during his supervised practicum, and his successful experiences with clients while practicing independently. It is also determined by the number of cases Jack has successfully treated. As you will read below, successful and independent behavior change is the hallmark of one's competence. As a whole, it is within Jack's *scope of practice* to take Theo on as a client. However, it is not within his *scope of competence.*

Compare Jack's background to Shanun's. Shanun is a BCBA who runs a center similar to Jack's. In Shanun's graduate program, she received extensive training through coursework and supervision in functional assessment and treatment of challenging behavior. Relatedly, her practicum supervisor was a leading expert in functional assessment who had published multiple papers in peer-reviewed journals on the topic. Shanun has treated a variety of different topographies of challenging behavior using a variety of function-based treatments. As a result, Shanun's *scope of practice* is in behavior analysis and her *scope of competence* is in functional assessment and treatment of challenging behavior. Shanun would have been an appropriately qualified professional to treat Theo.

IDENTIFYING YOUR OWN SCOPE OF COMPETENCE

The field of Applied Behavior Analysis (ABA) has not decided on many formal guidelines to identify one's scope of competence.[2] Currently, guidance comes from the BACB Code (Guideline 1.02) and

---

[2]For historical perspective, the BACB undertook a study in 2006-2007 to explore the possibly of adopting specialty certificates, but such action was not pursued (BACB, 2007).

licensure laws, where applicable. As highlighted with the example of Jack and Theo, the BACB Code is general and tells BCBAs *that* they should remain within their scope of competence—not *how* to remain within their scope of competence. As a result, the field is still at a point where it is the responsibility of each individual BCBA to define his or her own scope of competence. It should be noted the topic of *scope of competence* itself has been polarizing and controversial in behavior analysis.

As with most behavior, identifying one's own scope of competence is a learned skill. Identifying one's scope of competence begins by analyzing your own *education, training*, and *supervised experience* by asking three questions:

1. What populations, specific behavioral topographies, and assessment/intervention procedures were covered in depth in my graduate coursework?
2. What populations and specific behavioral topographies have I successfully implemented assessment/intervention procedures with under the supervision of a competent BCBA?
3. What populations and specific behavioral topographies have I successfully and independently implemented assessment/intervention procedures with in a clinical setting?

You should be able to identify your scope of competence once the above three questions have been answered by you or a trusted colleague (e.g., your practicum supervisor, a senior colleague). In addition, analyzing one's scope of competence is an ongoing task. What was once outside of one's competence may someday fall within one's competence. Similarly, what was once within one's competence may someday fall outside one's competence due to lack of practice or not keeping up with advances in the field (Fig. 4.1).

WHAT COURSEWORK EXPERIENCES DEFINE MY SCOPE OF COMPETENCE?

As the BACB has stated, coursework plays a role in defining one's scope of competence. One type of relevant coursework is population specific. For example, coursework in behavioral interventions for autism treatment would improve competence in autism treatment. Likewise, individuals who receive academic instruction focusing on adolescents and

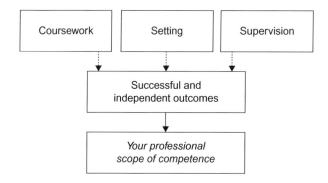

Figure 4.1 A conceptual framework for identifying your own scope of competence.

adults with autism may be more competent to serve clients in those populations, as opposed to an individual whose coursework specializes primarily in early childhood. And, training with any of the above would not indicate competence to work in Organizational Behavior Management (OBM) or with individuals with substance use difficulties.

Setting specific coursework is also relevant when defining one's scope of competence. For example, individuals in special education programs will likely experience coursework in educational law and policy improving their competence to work with children with autism in public schools. Likewise, coursework in OBM would improve competence in OBM. Though someone may experience coursework in employee training in autism delivery, this coursework, by itself, would limit their scope of competence to employee training in that area. For example, it would be unlikely the coursework in training employees in autism service delivery would also make the individual competent to train employees in a manufacturing setting, a sports marketing firm, or to implement a therapeutic workplace for drug addicts.

A final area of relevant coursework is procedure specific. These courses included topics such as assessment (e.g., functional assessment, preference assessment), interventions (e.g., differential reinforcement, positive-behavior supports), research methods (e.g., within-subject designs, group designs), and data analysis (e.g., visual inspection, quantitative analyses). It is unlikely every relevant topic a BCBA will ever confront in their practice was discussed in sufficient detail within the limited instructional time available for each of these areas. As a result, each of our scope of competence is limited to some degree within each of these areas.

WHAT EXPERIENCES IN VARIOUS SETTINGS DEFINE MY SCOPE OF COMPETENCE?

The setting-specific training you receive also plays a role in defining your scope of competence. For example, BCBAs will learn different legal considerations that allow one to competently work within a specific setting. Consider an individual who receives training in a public-school setting. This person is likely to learn about state and federal laws that affect implementation of behavioral principles in that setting (e.g., Individuals with Disabilities Education Act). In contrast, an individual who is trained in a private center-based program may never need to learn public education laws or how they impact implementation of behavioral interventions. But, the individual trained in a private center-based program may become intimately familiar with state laws regarding behavior analysis as a *medically necessary treatment* for autism—a topic never discussed in the teacher's lounge at school. Both behavior analysts subsequently have different scopes of competence when it comes to the settings in which behavioral treatment is implemented.

Setting-specific training also impacts scope of competence with instructional design. The private center-based BCBA may learn how to competently design interventions using small student-to-instructor ratios. However, they may not be competent designing and implementing classroom wide behavior change programs (e.g., the Good Behavior Game; Groves & Austin, 2017). In contrast, the BCBA trained in the public-school setting likely is competent in designing and implementing classroom wide behavior change programs but may not be proficient designing the most effective 1-to-1 therapy sessions.

Public education and center-based programs are only two examples of settings in which autism treatment occurs. Home-based programs, community-based programs, residential treatment facilities, and vocational settings are some of the many other training settings that differentially affect a professional's scope of competence. Each setting has its own unique context that shapes the knowledge, skills, and abilities of a professional's individual scope of competence.

WHAT SUPERVISION EXPERIENCES DEFINE MY SCOPE OF COMPETENCE?

The BACB has instituted a number of initial and ongoing requirements for professionals who wish to provide supervision to those pursing a

BCBA credential. However, these requirements do not guarantee that a supervisor of a professional pursuing certification, or supervising a BCBA postcertification, will engage in best-practice supervisory techniques. Falender and Shafranske (2012) astutely remind us of this fact, noting that "[s]ince clinical supervision is now widely acknowledged as a distinct professional practice, it is no longer assumed that competence as a supervisor is accomplished through osmosis" (p. 133).

What does this mean for your own scope of competence? In all likelihood, the better your supervisor was at supervising you, the more competent you will be in implementing clinical procedures with the targeted population in the setting he or she supervised you in. Luckily, recommended supervisory behaviors have already been described in the published literature (Sellers, Valentino, & LeBlanc, 2016).

The ability to effectively supervise is only one skill a supervisor possesses. The supervisor also is hopefully competent implementing different clinical procedures with specific populations and within specific settings. As a result, the boundaries of your supervisor's competence help define your own scope of competence. For example, some BCBAs are only competent in functional assessment and treatment of severe behavior. Others of us are competent in early intensive behavioral intervention (EIBI) for children younger than three years old. Each of us can only adequately train others in behavior analytic skills we are already competent in. Accordingly, you have only been adequately trained in the areas your supervisor was competent.

CONSIDER YOUR ANSWERS IN THE CONTEXT OF SUCCESSFUL TREATMENT OUTCOMES

In the previous section, we provided three questions to ask yourself about components that affect your scope of competence. In addition to the BACB's definition of competence, we added an additional and necessary component. Each BCBA's competence is determined by his or her previous experiences in demonstrating successful behavior change. Put another way, even if you received the best coursework in EIBI, conducted your field experience in an incredible EIBI classroom, and were supervised by a highly skilled supervisor who specialized in EIBI, you can only say you are competent in EIBI if you have independently and successfully produced behavior change in EIBI.

In an ideal world, independent demonstration of successful behavior change would be observed and measured by someone other than oneself (e.g., a highly qualified supervisor or consultant). You would not send your car to a mechanic for a transmission change if the mechanic had never changed a transmission and was not supervised by someone who had. You would not send your father-in-law to an orthopedic surgeon for a hip replacement if that surgeon had never replaced a hip and was not supervised by someone who had. You should not expect your clients to be exposed to your assessment or intervention procedures if you have never successfully implemented them before or are not supervised by someone who has.

HOW TO BROADEN YOUR SCOPE OF COMPETENCE

The first step to broadening competence is to recognize that you need to broaden your competence. The second step is to find a qualified supervisor with extensive experience in an area you are interested in learning about. The third step is to outline the skills and timeline you are seeking to complete supervision within. This may include specific goals such as learning to implement contingency management for increasing physical activity in individuals with developmental disabilities by next Thursday. Or, the goals may be broad such as learning by the end of the year about the history behind contingency management and current best practice for implementing it with many different behavioral topographies. Finally, you and the potential supervisor will need to determine compensation and sign a formal contract.

Sometimes there are no qualified supervisors with extensive experience in the area you want to learn about. For these instances, we refer readers to an article published by LeBlanc, Heinicke, and Baker (2009). In that article, the authors provide detailed recommendations for branching into new areas in behavior analysis. These include activities such as contacting the relevant literature and professional groups, and pursuing additional certifications or credentials.

WHEN TO SEEK ADDITIONAL TRAINING AND WHEN TO REFER A CLIENT

In the story at the beginning of this chapter, Jack was clearly in over his head. Though Jack should not have accepted Theo as a client in the first place, Jack had to decide what to do when he realized he was failing to make progress with Theo. Generally, two options are available. Jack could seek additional supervision and training to become competent himself. Or, Jack can refer Theo to a BCBA who is competent to help Theo.

Deciding between the two options depends on time and severity. The BCBA needs to determine how long it will be until the benefits and reduced harm will result from Jack's competent intervention. These include questions such as: how long will it take Jack to become competent? How long will Theo continue to behave aggressively and put himself and others at risk? How much physical damage is Theo causing with his aggression (e.g., Iwata, Pace, Kissel, Nau, & Farber, 1990)? How long will Theo continue to masturbate in public settings putting himself and others at risk? How long will it be until Theo benefits from the services provided to him by Jack?

Jack should likely keep Theo as a client if answers about time and severity are low. That is, Jack may consider keeping Theo as a client if the amount of time it will take Jack to become competent or to implement an intervention supervised by a competent individual will occur within days. Or, Jack may consider keeping Theo as a client if the aggressive behavior is infrequent and only results in red or irritated areas with no breaks in the skin (i.e., low severity).

Jack should likely refer Theo to a competent BCBA if answers about time and severity are high. That is, Jack should refer Theo to another BCBA if additional consultation or training will result in significant improvement only after several months, or if the aggression is so severe that you cannot wait a day or two for additional consultation and training. It is always difficult to recognize and confront the limits of one's abilities. Especially when we are often successful with so many clients. However, your client can only benefit by you saying, "I am not qualified to handle this," "I have bitten off more than I can chew," and "This client needs an expert." BACB Guideline 2.0 states that "behavior analysts have a responsibility to act in the best interest of clients." We know of no better way to fulfill this obligation than by accurately recognizing one's scope of competence.

A NEED FOR AN HONEST EVALUATION

Throughout our professional experiences, we have often heard the following (and similar) phrases muttered by even the most well-intentioned BCBAs: "I'm the client's best chance for success"; "There's nobody to refer the client to who will do as good a job as I can"; and "The client will fail if we do not accept him/her as a client." Assuming these comments are well intentioned and we can cast aside questions about accuracy, the decision whether to accept a client outside one's scope of competence is a complicated ethical issue.

In one potential situation, other appropriate ABA providers exist within a practical geographical range of the client. In these situations it is helpful to reflect on whether your motives to accept or continue to treat the client are based on objective data about your abilities relative to other BCBAs, or your own subjective opinion. Put another way, how do you know you are the best game in town for this particular client? What are the strengths and weaknesses of other ABA providers in your area? How do you know that to be so? Instead of treating the case on your own, this situation may present an ideal opportunity to learn about and establish cooperative and collaborative relationships with other providers in your area. No one is great at everything. By appropriately referring to other providers, you may set yourself up for future *referrals* from them in your areas of strength. And, the clients and larger community will be better served as a result.

In a more difficult situation, other appropriate ABA providers do not exist within a practical geographical range of the client. That is, you or your organization *really* are the best option. But, accepting or continuing to treat the client would cause you to practice outside of your scope of competence. This is likely an ethical dilemma. BACB Guideline 1.02b requires you obtain proper training or supervision *prior* to providing treatment. However, this conflicts with the responsibility you have to operate in the best interest of your client (BACB Code Section 2.0)—providing *some* service may be better than *no* service. Additionally, the minimal benefit gained for this client has to be balanced with the likely greater benefit gained for a different client within your scope of competence but that you cannot serve by taking on the first client.

In the ideal situation, the BCBA would work with the family to delay the onset of services until appropriate supervision and training could be obtained. However, sometimes this may not be possible (e.g., the client engages in severe self-injury that needs immediate attention or the client and their family speaks and understands only Klingon). In this situation, we do not have a recommended action. Many factors may influence which Guideline to follow. If you decide to serve the client, it seems to go without saying that you would have to make a continuous effort to access additional training and supervision to support treatment for that client. Relatedly, Guideline 1.04a would continuously reign supreme. You should be honest with the client and/or their caregivers about your limitations and your efforts to ensure they are receiving appropriate and effective ABA services.

CHAPTER SUMMARY

We hope this chapter provided you with one perspective for how a BCBA may define his or her own scope of competence and how scope of competence relates to a BCBA's scope of practice. Though the case study discussed in this chapter covers only a portion of what it may mean to be competent, we hope it helps you in your practice. We all have strengths and limitations in our abilities. What are yours? We also hope you encourage others to be aware of their own scope of competence. At the agency level, we hope everyone recognizes the limitations of their training, pursue additional training where needed, and refer clients to more qualified professionals when appropriate. In sum, engaging in an honest analysis of one's *scope of competence* will allow you to allocate your time and attention to clients you are best trained to serve. After all, they are entitled to nothing less than the most-effective treatment implemented by a competent provider (Van Houten et al., 1988).

QUESTIONS TO HELP YOU INCORPORATE THIS CHAPTER INTO YOUR PRACTICE

1. How do the definitions of *scope of practice* and *scope of competence* relate to Continuing Education (CE) requirements for BCBAs?
2. Have you ever been asked to practice outside of your *scope of competence*? How did you manage that situation? How would you manage that situation differently if you were asked to practice outside of your *scope of competence* in the future?
3. What educational experiences (e.g., courses, reading groups) have you had that provide evidence of your competence? What topics and populations were covered in those experiences?
4. What supervision experiences have you had that provide evidence of your competence? With what skills, populations, and settings

were you supervised? Looking back, what areas of ABA did your supervisor have little to no expertise with? Have you practiced in any of those areas in the past month?

5. What clinical experiences have you had postcertification that provide evidence for your competence with certain clinical skills, populations, or settings? How do you know you are competent in these areas? Would you consider yourself an expert in any areas of ABA? How do you know you are?

6. Look at your answers to questions 3–5. Now pick up an issue of *your favorite behavior-analytic journal.* What topics/populations/settings are reported on where you have received little-to-no training? What areas/populations/settings are reported on that you gained experience with only after you became a BCBA? What areas/populations/settings do you want to be competent in? How will you become competent?

7. How many service providers live in your surrounding area? What are the clinical strengths and weaknesses of those agencies? How do your clinical strengths and weaknesses contrast with theirs? Are you collaborating with other agencies to create a network of providers with varied expertise to better support your community? If not, why aren't you?

8. Think of the clients that have come to your agency in the last year where you struggled to provide effective services. What made these cases difficult? What skills would have helped you better serve these clients? What have you done to gain those skills in the past year? If there are struggles that have repeated themselves over the past year, is this an opportunity for expanding your business?

CHAPTER 5

The Decision-Making Process of Evidence-Based Practice

"It may not be science which is wrong but only its application."

—B.F. Skinner

What do an Old Testament prophet, an 18th century British navy doctor, and an "improper Bostonian" have in common? They each contributed to the development of evidence-based *medicine* (Claridge & Fabian, 2005). Each compared different treatment methods and concluded the treatment with the best outcome should be used in future practice. Each sought to use objective evidence as the basis for making clinical practice decisions.

Behavior analysts have promoted *evidence-based practice* (EBP) as a central component of Applied Behavior Analysis (ABA) for decades (Lindsley, 1990; Skinner, 1953; Van Houten et al., 1988). However, what does EBP even mean? Is EBP merely a Board Certified Behavior Analyst (BCBA) implementing a procedure as published in the pages of the *Journal of Applied Behavior Analysis*? What about an assessment, like functional analysis (FA; Beavers, Iwata, & Lerman, 2013)? A robust body of research supports FA as the most effective procedure for identifying the function of behavior. Does the size of this body of literature suggest EBP *requires* FAs to be conducted? Or is "require" too strong of a word and FAs are just "recommended"? What about the unique and unpublished intervention you designed for your client? If the logic of the intervention is sound, and the procedures and rationale are based on behavioral principles, is it still an EBP? Or, is EBP just another buzzword that has been thrown around so much that nobody really knows what it means? Look around you. EBP is used daily in the media, online, and even case-conference meetings. In a lot of ways, EBP may appear to be another fad likely to pass, like dabbing and fidget spinners.

Practical Ethics for Effective Treatment of Autism Spectrum Disorder. DOI: https://doi.org/10.1016/B978-0-12-814098-7.00005-5

In this chapter, we hope to shed some light on what EBP is and is not. This is a large undertaking for a single chapter, and our discussion is limited. For a book length analysis and discussion of EBP, we refer readers to Wilczynski (2017). Here, we first review how EBP has been defined in medicine and psychology to provide historical context and more recent discussion within behavior analysis. We then discuss recent disagreement within behavior analytic literature on how to define EBP in ABA. In the end, we promote the view that EBP is a process—not just using a treatment that has research to support it. Viewing EBP as a process, rather than single act, allows behavior analysts to fulfill their obligation to numerous Guidelines from the Behavior Analyst Certification Board (BACB) Code. In Table 5.1, we have provided a list and description of the BACB Code Guidelines that are relevant to the practice and process of EBP in ABA.

Table 5.1 Brief Description of the BACB Codes Related to the Definition of EBP. Specifically, the BACB Code Requires BCBAs to Identify and Use the Best Available Research, Establish and Practice Within His/Her Clinical Expertise, and to Respect Client Values, Preferences, Characteristics, Circumstances	
Code	Description
1.01 Reliance on Scientific Knowledge	Behavior analysts rely on scientific knowledge and practices when choosing and implementing treatment (i.e., best available research evidence). However, there are a plethora of views for defining what constitutes scientific knowledge (e.g., Smith, 2013).
1.02 Boundaries of Competence	Behavior analysts provide services commensurate with education, training, and supervised experience (i.e., clinical competence).
1.05b,c Professional and Scientific Relationships	Behavior analysts respect client values, preferences, characteristics, and circumstances by using language that is fully understandable, but conceptually systematic. Differences of age, gender, race, culture, ethnicity, national origin, religion, etc., are respected.
2.01 Accepting Clients	Behavior analysts support only those individuals with whom they have the clinical expertise to support. Or, they seek appropriate supervision and professional while supporting the individual.
2.04 Third-Party Involvement in Services	Behavior analytic services are often requested by a third-party (e.g., parent for a child, school for a student, business for employees). The behavior analyst must identify the values, preferences, characteristics, and circumstances for all parties involved, and which party is the "client" so that the best interest of the client can be maintained.
2.05 Rights and Prerogatives of Clients	Behavior analysts support client rights. One identified client right is effective treatment (Van Houten et al., 1989).

(Continued)

Table 5.1 (Continued)	
Code	**Description**
2.09 Treatment/Intervention Efficacy	Behavior analysts must advocate for and educate about scientifically supported, most effective treatment procedures (i.e., long-term and short-term benefits). Tools such as the NAC Standards Reports (2009) may provide some guidance in this effort; but, as pointed out by Smith (2013), have limitations to consider. Behavior analysts should consider client preference in context of all treatment options, not just when two or more scientifically supported treatments are available.
3.01 Behavior Analytic Assessment	The type of assessment is guided by client needs, environmental parameters, and other contextual variables. Some of these "contextual variables" are understood by knowing client values, preferences, characteristics, and circumstances (e.g., Fong et al., 2016).
4.02 Involving Clients in Planning and Consent	Involvement of the client should include understanding of client values, preferences, characteristics, and circumstances.
4.03 Individualized Behavior-Change Programs	Behavior-change programs consider the unique behaviors, environmental variables, assessment results, and goals of each client. This individualization is guided by client values, preferences, characteristics, and circumstances.
4.06 Describing Conditions for Behavior-Change Program Success	Behavior analysts might interpret this Code as a need to change the typical environment to match research conditions to ensure success. We encourage behavior analysts to also consider long-term success (see Code 2.09) when considering environmental conditions for success. Recent work has suggested changes in treatment conditions may lead to resurgence of behaviors requiring treatment (e.g., Peterson et al., 2017; Podlesnik, Kelley, Jimenez-Gomez, & Bouton, 2017; Wacker, et al., 2013).
4.07 Environmental Conditions that Interfere with Implementation	As with Code 4.06, behavior analysts are directed to alter the environment that prevent implementation of behavior-change programs. This focus on changing the environment without consideration of changing the behavior-change program does not give consideration to client values, preferences, characteristics, and circumstances. We encourage behavior analysts to consider the behavior-change program might be a barrier to success, not just the environment in which it is implemented. Novel application of behavior-change programs can also inform evidence-based practices and research agendas.
4.09 Least Restrictive Procedures	When determining scientifically supported treatments, behavior analysts should give preference to the least restrictive interventions.

DEFINITIONS FROM MEDICINE AND PSYCHOLOGY

We will start by taking a step back to review where the definition of EBP came from. Like many aspects of behavior analysis, the fields of medicine and psychology have influenced how BCBAs have come to define what EBP is and is not. In medicine, EBP has been defined as a process that involves the "conscientious, explicit, judicious use of current best evidence in making decisions about the care of the individual" (Sacket, Rosenberg, Gray, Haynes, & Richardson, 1996). An important component of this definition is emphasis on *current best evidence* to guide treatment decisions.

Other components of this definition may create a problem. The problem is that engaging in the behaviors that Sacket et al. (1996) define as representing *conscientious, explicit*, and *judicious use of evidence* may not allow a professional to balance the values of a client, as well as that professional's own background, when making a treatment decision. As we will discuss in a bit, client values and professional expertise are also important to EBP. Despite the limitations of this definition, it remains helpful because it highlights that an important component of EBP is how one *uses evidence*.

Strauss, Glasziou, Richardson, and Haynes (2011) provide a more complete definition of EBP. They note that evidence-based medicine "requires the integration of the best research evidence with our clinical expertise and our patient's[1] unique values and circumstances." This definition emphasizes three components of evidence-based medicine: *research evidence, professional expertise*, and *client characteristics*. Strauss and colleagues emphasize that EBP is a process. This process involves not only evaluating *research evidence*, but integrating this evidence with *professional expertise, client characteristics*, and *input from various stakeholders* (e.g., caregivers).

It is again important to emphasize the process-orientated nature of EBP. It is unlikely a published research study exists that describes the specific problem you face and the client you are facing it with. You will necessarily have to use your past clinical experiences and input from those around you to make ongoing decisions for each unique client. The definition from Strauss and colleagues highlights that EBP is not a one-time decision (e.g., I chose to use functional communication training, or not). Rather, EBP is a continuous process of finding available published research evidence, assessing collected data from the treatment program, and obtaining and assessing contextual information unique to your client (e.g., information from caregivers and staff).

[1]We recognize there are multiple terms to describe an individual receiving treatment, and they are often different across human service disciplines. We have opted to use the term "client" throughout the chapter, unless referencing a specific aspect of service from another discipline.

To summarize, Strauss et al. promote three components of EBP: (1) research evidence, (2) clinical expertise, and (3) client considerations. All three are utilized to make a clinical decision. All three components are critical to the EBP process.

THE THREE-LEGGED STOOL ANALOGY

The defining characteristics of EBP and equal importance of each component can be helpfully illustrated with an analogy (Spring, 2007). Picture an old, rustic wood cabin nestled quietly in the thick maple forest of Michigan's Upper Peninsula. Passed down from generation to generation, the cabin is small, cozy, and furnished with old wool blankets and dusty photographs of forgotten relatives. In the corner of that cabin sits a three-legged stool, handmade from the same maple trees that surround the cabin. The stool is old, though it is strong and sturdy.

Each leg of the stool represents one component of EBP. One leg represents the *best available evidence*, one leg represents *clinical expertise*, and the final leg represents *client values, preferences, characteristics, and circumstances*. If all three of those legs are strong and of equal height, then that stool will continue to support you. If all three of those legs are strong and of equal height, then EBP should result in successful client outcomes. If one or more of those legs are weak or of different height, then that stool will topple and send you flying into the cardboard box of dusty Northwoods Readers. If any one leg is absent or weak, EBP is either weak or may not be occurring, and your treatment is unlikely to achieve optimal outcomes (Spring, 2007).

DEFINING EVIDENCE-BASED PRACTICE
IN APPLIED BEHAVIOR ANALYSIS

Behavior analytic researchers have also offered definitions of what EBP might mean in ABA. Two of these views were put forth by Smith (2013) and Slocum and colleagues (2014). The definitions of EBP in psychology and medicine, along with the three-legged stool analogy, can provide context for understanding these definitions of EBP in ABA.

Manualized Procedures Validated Through Research
One definition of EBP in ABA was provided by Smith (2013):

> ... an evidence-based practice is a service that helps to solve a consumer's problem. Thus, it is likely to be an integrated package of procedures, operationalized in a manual, and validated in studies of socially meaningful outcomes, usually with group designs (p. 27).

Smith's definition is important because it emphasizes *manualized procedures* validated through research. For example, the Picture Exchange Communication System (PECS) is an example of one manualized set of procedures. The procedures of PECS aim at establishing the foundational skills of selection-based augmentative and alternative communication (Bondy & Frost, 1994). The PECS manual contains a series of skills that are broken into discrete steps and components that are easy for the supervising clinician to follow. The BCBA is supposed to follow the steps and components precisely as they are outlined in the manual because that is the process that has been supported through research. Anything else, "is not PECS."

Another example of a manualized procedure is the University of California at Los Angeles Young Autism Project method, commonly known as the UCLA Model (see Reichow & Wolery, 2009). The UCLA Model uses a manualized intervention guide (Lovaas Institute, 2003) to help organize, deliver, and troubleshoot behavioral treatment. For example, the UCLA Model provides specific instructions for how the supervising clinician should do x and y. In contrast to PECS which addresses a subset of skills (e.g., speech and language), the UCLA Model addresses a more global range of skills.

Both PECS and the UCLA Model are operationalized manuals containing packaged procedures. The final step for these to meet Smith's (2013) definition of EBP is for PECS and the UCLA Model to be validated as producing socially meaningful outcomes. That is, PECS and the UCLA Model would need to be: evaluated in multiple contexts, implemented by multiple interventionists—such as teachers and clinicians, and be evaluated using high-quality research methodology. Smith's definition of an EBP implies an interventionist could purchase a manual and implement the procedures in the manual. If followed correctly, this would result in the desired behavior change.

EVIDENCE-BASED PRACTICE AS
A DECISION-MAKING PROCESS

Tim Slocum and colleagues (2014; also see Wilczynski, 2017) offered a contrasting definition of EBP. Namely, Smith's definition emphasized "practice" within EBP as a service provided to consumers. Such emphasis closely resembles a distinction between EBP and *evidence supported treatment* put forth by the American Psychological Association Presidential Task Force (2006). Evidence-supported treatment is often confused with EBP, but they are not the same.

An evidence-supported treatment is an intervention that has been shown through research to be effective with a given population. For example, a researcher may publish a study that evaluates the effects of the PECS manual in improving language outcomes for children with autism in multiple community-based settings across the United States. Positive results of that study would imply the PECS manual is an evidence-supported treatment for children with autism.

Evidence-supported treatments lack crucial components of EBP. The first critical missing component is professional expertise. For example, though research may suggest the PECS manual is effective, the competence of the interventionist will affect the fidelity in which the manual is implemented and the degree of behavior change that will occur (the effectiveness of the intervention). Research provides evidence of efficacy, whereas professional expertise affects effectiveness (as discussed in our chapter on scope of competence). Any geek off the street is unable pick up the PECS manual, implement it, and expect positive outcomes. Instead, that person must be competent in all the clinical skills that are required within the PECS manual. The evidence-supported treatment paradigm, whether intentional or not, fails to explicitly include clinical expertise within the EBP paradigm.

A second critical missing component is integration of client values, preferences and characteristics. Integrating client values, preferences, and characteristics is important because these affect things like treatment selection and adherence to treatment protocols. Values and preferences include things such as a client's cultural background, their current family environment, and their availability to access financial resources. Client characteristics may include things like their disability, the severity of that disability, comorbid diagnoses, and individual skill deficits and strengths. These will impact intervention delivery and need to be considered as imperative to EBP in ABA (Slocum et al., 2014).

Slocum and colleagues (2014) offer a different definition of EBP that incorporates *professional expertise* and *client values, preferences, and characteristics*. Specifically, their definition reads as follows:

Evidence-based practice of applied behavior analysis is a decision-making process that integrates (a) the best available evidence with (b) clinical expertise and (c) client values and context (p. 44).

This definition is very similar to those proposed in the medical (Strauss, Glasziou, Richardson, & Haynes, 2011) and psychological (APA, 2006) professions. This definition also closely resembles that of the three-legged stool analogy described by Spring (2007). Importantly, Slocum et al.'s definition of EBP also implies that *EBP is a process*.

USING EVIDENCE-BASED PRACTICE IN APPLIED BEHAVIOR ANALYSIS

To implement the process of EBP in ABA, each leg of the analogic stool must support the weight placed on it. Each leg must be strong, sturdy, solid, and of equal height. Below (see Fig. 5.1), we describe how behavior analysts can ensure each leg supports its weight. In particular, we focus on identifying the best available evidence as well as client considerations. Clinical expertise is discussed only briefly because we covered it in Chapter 4, Identifying Your Scope of Competence in Autism Treatment. Following descriptions of the three components of EBP— *research evidence, clinical expertise,* and *client considerations*—we provide a few case studies that illustrate the process of EBP in ABA. As stated previously, we encourage readers to review Wilczynski (2017) for a more in-depth discussion regarding EBP in ABA.

IDENTIFYING THE BEST AVAILABLE EVIDENCE

As we mentioned earlier, an evidence-supported treatment is a treatment that has been empirically demonstrated to be effective. But how do you find evidence-supported treatments in ABA? Given the time constraints you may face as a practicing BCBA, how can you stay abreast of changes and advancements in evidence-supported treatments? Furthermore, how do you deal with the barriers associated

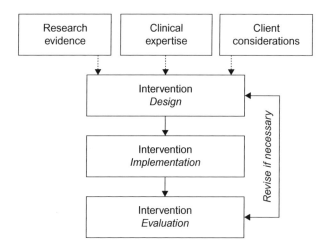

Figure 5.1 The process of evidence-based practice in Applied Behavior Analysis.

with locating research, such as accessing costly research databases? And once you have that evidence, how do you make sense of it? Luckily, there are multiple ways to locate, and make sense of, evidence-supported treatments.

Identification of a Clinical Problem

One strategy to identify an evidence-supported treatment is to begin by identifying the relevant clinical problem. Then, you conduct a structured search, based on that problem, which culminates in the identification and implementation of an evidence-supported treatment (Strauss et al., 2011). For example, you may notice that one of your clients has trouble staying on-task for extended lengths of time. Through a structured search, you are likely to come across research supporting activity schedules or demand fading as treatments for improving on-task behavior.

The benefit of this *clinical problem*-based approach is that the search technique is specific to the problem at hand. The downside to this approach is that clinicians may become good at treating a certain clinical problem in a certain way. As a result, they may fail to learn about new and better treatments that arise in the future. In addition, BCBAs may inadvertently learn to address certain topographies of behavior only with certain procedures. Thus they would fail to develop a larger, overarching clinical repertoire of identifying and designing treatments across multiple topographies and settings.

Accessing the literature only when clinical problems arise could potentially hinder the BCBA's skill acquisition and result in a limited skill set.

Regular Contact With the Research Literature

A second strategy is to maintain regular contact with all or most of the research literature. Regular contact is made independent of a specific clinical problem. To maintain contact, you may subscribe to relevant journals in your field, consistently visit the Web site of relevant journals to review newly published articles, or attend a journal reading group.

The benefit of this strategy is that it allows you to stay current with advances in treatment options and incorporate better interventions as soon as they become available. Downsides to this approach are the time it may take to remain current with updates, and limited or no access to relevant literature once found (Carr & Briggs, 2010; Spring, 2007; Weinberger, 2011). In addition, many BCBAs working with non traditional populations may not publish behavior analytic research in common ABA journals (e.g., Dallery, Glenn, & Raiff, 2007; Petry, Andrade, Barry, & Byrne, 2013). This can increase the difficulty of finding and subscribing to journals that publish relevant evidence-supported treatments.

Organizational Efforts

The above strategies can be applied and expanded upon within an organization (Quigley & Weiss, 2017). An organization may purchase[2] access to a research database and provide BCBAs with information on different ways to access research literature (e.g., clinical meetings, professional organizations, conferences, continuing education, contacting authors). Organizations may also coordinate monthly meetings that discuss how recently published literature relates to the practices they engage in at that organization.

Organizational efforts to provide employees with access to research may increase the efficiency in accessing and contacting updates to research literature. Efficiency is improved because the responsibilities of keeping current can be spread among multiple people. In addition,

[2]We wish to thank the BACB for providing database access for BCBAs. We have personally benefitted from this resource. We encourage all BCBAs to utilize this free service.

the resources of an organization are likely greater than the resources any one employee has. Greater resources for accessing the literature increases the likelihood that relevant content will be found. One potential downside to this approach is that it can be costly to purchase organizational subscriptions to research databases. In addition, time spent discussing research articles may not transfer to billable hours. Therefore companies will not profit from time spent on professional development alone, and it may even come at a cost.

EVALUATING EVIDENCE ONCE YOU FIND IT

Not all evidence is created equal. You must remain cognizant of what it takes to critically evaluate evidence, and this evaluation will take the form of one of three different courses of action.

The BCBA Practitioner as a Researcher, Now and Forever

A search of the evidence may fail to yield any relevant results or the results may be weak. If this occurs, the BCBA will have to play the role of a *researcher* and evaluate treatment options using an appropriate within-subject research design. That is, follow the analytic core feature of ABA (Baer, Wolf, & Risley, 1968). There is nothing more powerful than the systematic demonstration that an intervention has worked with a specific client. Therefore a BCBA may need to function as a researcher when no evidence is available to guide them (in the sense of carefully and empirically evaluating treatment, not necessarily publishing data).

The BCBA Practitioner as a Synthesizer

A search may also yield numerous publications of varying quality. In these instances, a BCBA should function as an evidence *synthesizer*. The role of a synthesizer requires the BCBA to use personal (e.g., professional knowledge of research methodology) or published criteria (e.g., National Autism Center—NAC, 2009) to evaluate the literature. Examples of these types of publications include reviews of specific procedures (e.g., SAFMEDS; Quigley, Peterson, Frieder, & Peck, 2017), procedures based upon a specific theory (e.g., sensory integration; Lang et al., 2012), and multiple procedures for a specific population (e.g., autism spectrum disorder; NAC, 2009, 2015; Wong et al., 2013). BCBAs seeking to maximize efficiency as a synthesizer could take advantage of already synthesized literature. Luckily, some organizations routinely publish summary reports about advancements within autism research (e.g., Interagency Autism Coordinating Committee—IACC, 2016).

The BCBA Practitioner as a User

The best-case scenario occurs when the available evidence closely aligns with the problem the BCBA faces. When this occurs, the BCBA can simply behave as a *user* of that information described in the research. For individual research articles, the BCBA should determine two things. First, how closely the relevant variables in the published research match their situation. Second, what changes need to be made to the intervention for the current case. If using already synthesized literature, BCBAs should be prepared to evaluate the quality and strength of that synthesized literature (Strauss et al., 2011).

INTEGRATING EVIDENCE WITH CLIENT CONSIDERATIONS

The process of EBP is not complete if client values, preferences, and characteristics are not taken into account. BCBAs can incorporate client values by remaining considerate of and actively dialoguing with clients about their culture and values before and while implementing behavioral interventions (BACB Code 1.05). Little is known about how behavioral intervention outcomes are influenced by cultural differences (e.g., client language, socioeconomic status, religious affiliations; Brodhead et al., 2014). Nevertheless, understanding and integrating cultural values seems likely to improve intervention outcomes. Incorporating values based on culture requires becoming culturally aware of one's own cultural values as well as the values of client's served (Fong et al., 2016).

BCBAs can integrate client preferences into EBP in several ways. One way is for the BCBA to verbally describe different treatment options and their likely outcomes (Spring, 2007). The client may then choose between the treatment options based on how they value different aspects of health. For clients with limited verbal capacity, such as those with autism, BCBAs may use a choice procedure similar to that described by Hanley and colleagues (2005). In this case, clients are given multiple opportunities to select between two or more treatment options. The most selected treatment is then considered to be the most preferred treatment for that client.

Finally, the BCBA needs to integrate client characteristics within the EBP process. Client characteristics include the skills and deficits of their particular client and how those skills and deficits align with relevant research. It is important to understand that no two people are alike. Published research reports data from participants who are different from your own clients in many ways. Though similarities may exist, you should recognize that many reported and unreported variables may affect how well an evidence-supported treatment is successful with your client (e.g., age, disability type, number of effective reinforcers).

INTEGRATING EVIDENCE WITH PROFESSIONAL EXPERTISE

BCBAs are required to practice within their boundaries of competence (BACB, 2014). As discussed in Chapter 4, Identifying Your Scope of Competence in Autism Treatment, one's scope of competence is affected by one's educational background, the settings one has practiced in, the supervision one has received, and the different clients one has worked with. As a result, each BCBA is more competent than other BCBAs in some areas. Relatedly, no BCBA is fully competent in all areas of ABA. Finally, we would argue each BCBA cannot be considered competent in an area unless he or she has independently demonstrated successful behavior change in that area (e.g., severe self-injurious behavior, feeding issues).

Whether one has competence in an area falls on a spectrum. That is, assessing one's competence is not answered with only a "yes" or "no." A BCBA must consider the degree of their own competence and how it may affect the EBP process. The more skilled the BCBA in a certain area, the more likely they can achieve optimal behavior change or successfully manage more complex cases in that area. The less skilled the BCBA in a certain area, the less likely they can achieve optimal behavior change or successfully manage more complex cases. In the latter instances, the process of EBP requires additional training or consultation in an amount commensurate with their lack of competence.

CASE STUDIES IN EBP IN ABA

In-home Therapy: EBP, You're Doing it Wrong

Cedar was a BCBA overseeing in-home therapy to Briar, a young woman with autism. Briar engaged in nearly constant aggressive behavior (hitting, scratching, & pinching) which impeded her ability to learn. In addition, Briar was about the same size as many staff. The Registered Behavior Technicians (RBTs) that worked with Briar were concerned about managing aggressive behavior for any duration of time.

Cedar began by finding evidence-supported treatments. Cedar began with a literature search using the term "aggression." In his search, he found multiple articles on how to treat aggression without having to use extinction as an intervention component (e.g., Athens & Vollmer, 2010; Peterson, Frieder, Smith, Quigley, & Van Norman, 2009). This was perfect considering the RBT's concerns about prolonged aggression of any kind!

Cedar was not much of an expert with problem behavior. But, the research study he found seemed similar enough to the problem he was facing. However, the participants in the published study displayed skill deficits that were much more severe than Briar's. Briar was considered very high-functioning and had very strong language and academic skills. However, Briar was not motivated to work unless it was on her own terms—which often included access to things Cedar could not actually get or use (e.g., liter of soda; trip to amusement park).

Cedar decided to use the DRA without extinction exactly as applied in the study. Cedar told the RBT who provided the daily in-home therapy to give Briar a high-quality break and attention when Briar asks for a break on her own. However, if Briar engaged in aggression, he asked the RBT to give her a low-quality break and attention. Other than his verbal instructions, Cedar did not train the therapist on any of the critical features of the procedure. A few weeks later, Cedar returned to the home, and Briar's aggression had not changed.

Analysis

The story of Cedar and Briar represents a failure to execute the process of EBP. Though Cedar did review the literature, he did so very briefly. As a result, he found studies that, though well-executed, parametrically evaluated components of behavioral treatments. By conducting the treatment in an identical manner, he failed to incorporate client characteristics and thus did not apply an EBP—as no evidence was given that delivery of a break and attention would be relevant with these client characteristics. Finally, Cedar failed to train the RBT and monitor the success of the intervention. Therefore Cedar's clinical expertise, or lack of, really shines in this classic example of an EBP fail.

EBP IN SPECIAL-EDUCATION: YOU'RE MISSING THE POINT

Christine was a BCBA and behavior consultant in a large public school. While attending an IEP for a student on her caseload, the student's teacher expressed concern that the student (Andrew) was having trouble completing his tasks on time and staying organized.

In an effort to help Andrew, Christine pulled up a Web site that had reviewed interventions for students with autism. Christine then interjected in the meeting and said, "It looks like video modeling will help. Video modeling is an EBP. We should implement video modeling." Everyone else at the meeting agreed, and Christine sent Andrew's teacher a link to the Web site and told her that she would order an iPad to use with Andrew.

A few months later, Christine went to visit Andrew in his classroom to follow up. Andrew was still having trouble completing tasks and his organization skills had gotten worse. The teacher reported that, though she had tried video modeling with Andrew, she had trouble maintaining Andrew's interest and the intervention required too much of her time.

Analysis

Christine's attempt at EBP is well-intentioned, but misunderstood. Though she was wise to review a resource that had provided excellent summary information about evidence-supported treatments, she did not take into account Andrew's individual characteristics (e.g., his interests), as well as the skills of Andrew's teacher (e.g., her ability to implement video modeling and still teach the rest of the students). Video modeling as an intervention was likely to be unsuccessful before it was ever implemented.

VOCATIONAL TRAINING: EBP DONE RIGHT[3]

Marisa is a BCBA who runs a program that provides behavioral services to young adults (ages 18–26) with developmental disabilities in entry-level vocational settings. Each adult works in a different setting. These settings include a coffee shop, cafeteria, and dairy store. Every work day, the adults meet with Marisa and then leave for their vocational setting. Marisa's program does not have the resources to drive every adult to work. Marisa also believes navigating transportation to work is an important independent living skill to develop.

Marisa searched the research literature and found studies that demonstrated how adults with developmental disabilities can learn to follow GPS-based software programs. However, this research only described how to use the software to *walk* somewhere. Marisa was unable to find research on using GPS to *ride the bus*. Fortunately, the participants in the studies were similar to the adults in her program so she inferred there would be some likelihood of similar success with the clients in her situation. In addition, Marisa knew the adults in her program enjoyed going to work and riding public transportation on the weekends (i.e., her goals and program were in line with the client's values and preferences). Finally, Marisa had previously and repeatedly demonstrated competence in designing instructional procedures to help adults with developmental disabilities learn self-management behavior for community settings in the past.

Analysis

Marisa designed a bus riding program for her adult clients by integrating available research evidence, her clients' values and preferences, and her own clinical expertise. Marisa monitored the effects of her intervention and made minor adjustments over time until her intervention was successful in teaching every adult to take public transportation. Marisa's intervention likely would have been less effective and failed to fit the definition of EBP if any of the three components were missing.

---

[3]This example is based on a study by Price, Marsh, and Fisher (2018).

CHAPTER SUMMARY

EBP has been defined differently by practitioners working across different areas of healthcare. When combined, these definitions cover three core attributes to the EBP process: the ability to find and evaluate evidence-supported interventions the ability to integrate published literature with client values and preferences; and the ability to integrate published literature with professional expertise. We offered several strategies relative to each of these areas. However, it should be noted there is little research to guide BCBAs on how to engage in EBP; improve their ability to use EBP; and integrate client values and preferences with their professional expertise. Each of these areas represent important areas for future research on ethical behavior of BCBAs.

QUESTIONS TO HELP YOU INCORPORATE THIS CHAPTER INTO YOUR PRACTICE

1. Why do the definitions of evidence-based practice from medicine and psychology (or other health professions) matter? How might definitions from other professions shape the way you speak to different audiences? How might definitions from other professions shape the way you write reports to insurance companies?
2. How have you defined/thought of evidenced based practice in the past? What aspects of the definitions provided by Smith (2013) and Slocum et al. (2014) did you fail to consider? What added dimensions do you think are missing from those definitions?
3. Are any lengths of the stool longer than the others in your clinical practice? That is, do you emphasize published evidence, professional expertise, or client values/preferences more than the other two? If so, how might you ethically justify those decisions (think back to Chapter 1)? If not, how might you ethically justify those decisions?
4. How do you currently access published evidence? How frequently do you access published evidence? How might behavioral systems analysis be used to improve your own and your organizations contact with published evidence?
5. How does the delay and probability of realizing outcomes from published procedures influence your decision to strictly adhere to published procedures? How does this process equate to or play a role in professional expertise?

6. When has your professional expertise led you to make a clinical or ethical decision that contrasts with published evidence? When has your professional expertise led you to make a clinical or ethical decision that contrasts with client preferences or values? How did you demonstrate that was the right course of action?

7. When have client preferences or values led you to make a clinical or ethical decision that contrasts with published evidence? When have client preferences or values led you to make a clinical or ethical decision that contrasts with your professional expertise? How did you demonstrate that was the right course of action?

8. Integrating available evidence, professional expertise, and client preferences/values is difficult. What systems do you have at your organization to help RBTs, BCaBAs, and BCBAs navigate these situations? What systems do you have at your organization to measure and evaluate how well everyone is navigating these situations?

CHAPTER 6

Interdisciplinary Collaboration

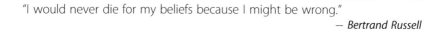

"I would never die for my beliefs because I might be wrong."
— *Bertrand Russell*

Public perception of Applied Behavior Analysis (ABA) can be fraught with misconceptions. How many times have you heard that reinforcement is bribery, or that Board Certified Behavior Analysts (BCBAs) use aversive techniques to force compliance in children with autism? How many times have you heard that BCBAs turn children with autism into robots and only conduct teaching in an isolated room at a tabletop? How many times have you heard that BCBAs fail to collaborate well with other professionals? If you have yet to hear these statements, and others like them, you likely are at the beginning of your career or have only worked with other BCBAs. Ask your instructor or a trusted professional who has been in the field for a while about misconceptions they have heard. They will likely have a number of experiences to share with you, or perhaps share some recently published papers on this topic (e.g., Barrett, 2015; Freedman, 2016; Smith, 2016).

Lucky for us, misconceptions about ABA are just that, misconceptions. Reinforcement is not bribery (Malott & Shane, 2014). Contemporary behavioral research on the treatment of autism has primarily focused on reinforcement-based interventions without having to resort to aversive techniques. Behavior Analyst Certification Board (BACB) Guideline 4.08 describes procedural safeguards for clients who require aversive procedures when reinforcement-only procedures are not effective. We have research that demonstrates teaching can occur anywhere and involve real-world skills (Dufek & Schreibman, 2014).

What we have little published literature on is how to collaborate with other professionals—particularly those from different disciplines

Practical Ethics for Effective Treatment of Autism Spectrum Disorder. DOI: https://doi.org/10.1016/B978-0-12-814098-7.00006-7

and ideologies. Therefore the statement that "BCBAs fail to collaborate well with other professionals" may be closer to the truth than we would like to admit. It may not be a misconception for some BCBAs.

By *collaboration*, we mean engaging in professional activities with another autism or related service provider to improve treatment outcomes. A more technical definition of collaboration is: "consultation involving voluntary, interpersonal interactions comprising of two or more professionals engaging in communication modalities (face-to-face meetings, e-mail, alternate means of feedback, etc.) for the purpose of shared decision-making and problem solving towards a common goal" (Kelly & Tincani, 2013, p. 124). An outcome of collaboration is that it "results in changes to tasks and solutions that would not have been achieved in isolation."

As Kelly and Tincani (2013) astutely point out, there are many component behaviors that make up the repertoire of "collaboration." In this chapter, we primarily discuss the component skill of "interpersonal interactions," or professional interactions, with all colleagues— behavior analysts or nonbehavior analysts. However, it should be recognized professional interactions are one of many likely components required for successful *interdisciplinary collaboration* (see Drotar & Sturm, 1996; MacDonald et al., 2010, for details on additional competencies).

You may ask, why are professional interactions so important, and what do they have to do with ethics? Professional interactions are a fundamental behavior-analytic skill (see BACB 4th and upcoming 5th edition Task Lists) and fall under our definition of ethical behavior (i.e., addressed in the BACB Code). For example, BACB Code 7.0 states that "[b]ehavior analysts work with colleagues within the profession of behavior analysis and from other professions..." High-quality professional interactions are expected of BCBAs.

Though professional interactions are extremely important, there is little behavior-analytic research on this topic. As a result, professors and supervisors in BCBA training programs have little empirical guidance for teaching professional interactions and other component skills of interdisciplinary collaboration. In a recent study a majority of the 302 BCBAs surveyed reported they received little to no training in collaboration during their undergraduate and graduate programs (Kelly

& Tincani, 2013). We find this concerning for two reasons. First, graduates from BCBA programs should be taught basics of professional interactions because they will be expected to competently engage in professional interactions once they are practicing independently. Second, the reality is that modern autism treatment continues to move toward multidisciplinary and/or interdisciplinary models of service provision (Cox, 2012).

What does this mean for you as a BCBA? It means you are likely to collaborate with Speech-Language Pathologists (SLPs), psychologists, occupational-therapists, special educators, physicians, and other human-service or medical professionals throughout the course of your career. Collaborating well with other professionals will allow you to improve client outcomes as well as meet the high standards of our profession (BACB Guideline 1.0). Specifically, engaging in appropriate professional interactions allows you to: operate with integrity (BACB Guideline 1.04), create and maintain high-quality professional and collaborative relationships (BACB Guideline 1.05, 2.03), minimize harm (BACB Guideline 4.10), and act in the best interest of the client (BACB Guideline 2.0). You will need to collaborate well with others.

RECOMMENDATIONS FOR PROFESSIONAL INTERACTIONS

Respect Cultural Differences

BACB Guideline 1.05 defines ethical requirements for the professional and scientific relationships which BCBAs have with their colleagues and clients. One major component of this specific guideline is that it describes *culture* as a key consideration. When differences in culture affect service delivery, those differences must be resolved. With regard to interdisciplinary collaboration, we interpret "culture" as the philosophical assumptions, guidelines (e.g., codes of ethics), and research that define a specific field or subfield of autism treatment.

ABA is a cultural system distinct from other cultures (Glenn, 1993). By cultural system, we mean ABA differs from other applied sciences because of the unique underlying philosophical assumptions and approach to research that guides the behavior of BCBAs. As one example, ABA emphasizes single-subject research. In contrast, other professional cultures value group-design studies. In another example, ABA values observable and measurable events as primary data and causal explanations. In contrast, other fields enjoy and embrace unobservable processes and hypothetical constructs as causal explanations. BCBAs, SLPs, Christians, Marxists, and Americans all have arranged social contingencies to describe and promote the collective ideals and behaviors expected by members of those groups. Each of these could be considered distinct cultures.

Treatment for individuals with autism is no different. Consider a situation where you need to collaborate with an SLP. They may adopt a cognitive perspective of language development and use terms like "mapping." The SLP also is unlikely to have read *Verbal Behavior* (Skinner, 1957) or be familiar with supporting research (DeSouza, Akers, & Fisher, 2017). Instead the SLP may read research and implement interventions described in journals outside what BCBAs are familiar with. Despite different theoretical frameworks and approaches to research, you and the SLP share the underlying goal of improving the verbal behavior of your shared client. The shared client will likely have improved verbal behavior outcomes if the BCBA is able to resolve differences and work toward common goals with the SLP (i.e., collaborate effectively; Rogers, Anthony, & Danley, 1989).

The first step to respecting the cultural differences of our colleagues is to learn about those differences. By learning about and appreciating the ideologies (e.g., backgrounds and worldviews) of your colleagues, you can better understand how their recommendations fit within the larger context of their goal of helping people with autism be successful. The more you understand their perspective, the more you may realize you both use different terms to describe similar things (Slocum & Butterfield, 1994).

RESPECT LEGAL, REGULATORY, AND POLICY BARRIERS

Collaborating with interdisciplinary professionals occurs within the boundaries of laws, regulations, and policies. Interdisciplinary professionals may each have their own code of ethics. Sometimes, these codes of ethics may not align with your own (Cox, 2018). For example, the code of ethics put forth by the Association of American Educators explicitly recognizes the role and importance of educators in the "moral education" of students (AAE, 2013). Educators adhering to this code of ethics may subsequently promote learning goals involving moral development which may be inappropriate to members of other professions. Relatedly the ability to practice as a member of some professions is regulated through compliance with the code of ethics (e.g., AOTA, 2015; ASHA, 2016; BACB, 2014). Resolving differences in ethical codes has to occur with an understanding of the regulations and policies to which other professionals will be held accountable.

Understanding legal requirements is another example of respecting culture to maximize treatment outcomes and act in the best interest of the client. For example, consider that Hugo, a BCBA, is at an Individualized Education Plan (IEP) meeting for Joe, a student for whom Hugo provides in-home ABA therapy. A special education teacher is also at the meeting. Special education teachers have a legal obligation to provide a *free* and *appropriate* public education for Joe. But, *free* and *appropriate* education does not come without constraints. Public education guidelines are heavily rooted in case law and legislative policy (e.g., the Supreme Court of the United State's 8-0 ruling in Endrew F. v. Douglas County School District). Public educators have to follow these laws. BCBAs that are not subjected to these regulations and are unaware of the constraints may feel the *free* and *appropriate* education promoted by a special educator is limited and less effective than it could be.

Effective collaboration will play out differently depending on whether Hugo understands the basic legal requirements of special education. Collaboration will be much more effective if Hugo understands that *free* and *appropriate* public education applies to fairly distributing limited resources among *all* students in the classroom. Thus, when the special education teacher says she can provide 15 min of one-on-one ABA per day to Joe, it does not mean the teacher thinks ABA is terrible or does not want to help Joe. It means the teacher is providing a *free* and *appropriate* public education for Joe based on the limited resources she has to divide among all students. This does not mean that BCBAs should not advocate for the time and resources they feel they need to be effective to meet their client's goals. In fact the BACB Code obligates BCBAs to note these barriers (Guideline 4.07). However, by recognizing the constraints and limitations the teacher may be under, the teacher and the BCBA can work collaboratively within resource constraints — rather than the BCBA feeling at odds with the teacher.

LIMIT TECHNICAL JARGON WHENEVER POSSIBLE

BCBAs use a lexicon of technical terms. *Operant, metonymical tact, mutual entailment,* and *surrogate-conditioned motivating operation* are just a few examples of the technical terms we love to toss around. Technical precision is a hallmark of our science and carries tremendous benefit (Baer, Wolf, & Risley, 1968). However, the benefits to precision through technical jargon are only gained by those who understand the language. There are several reasons excessive use of jargon can negatively impact your role in a treatment team.

First, you may confuse those around you by excessively using jargon. Unless your colleagues came straight out of a behavior analytic graduate program, they likely are not going to understand what you are talking about when you say "tact" instead of "label." This may be true for many of the technical terms we regularly use. Arguably, using less precise terms (to us) may result in greater precision in understanding (for others). As Dr. Rick Olenchak stated, "terms of little meaning to recipients of communication equate to imprecision" (personal communication, 2017). Precision is relative to the listener and their history with different words—not necessarily just the speaking BCBA. Put simply, there is little point in speaking if the person you are talking to cannot understand what you are saying. Over-using jargon is one way to ensure misunderstanding.

Second, you may also alienate yourself from the treatment team by excessively using jargon. Becirevic, Critchfield, and Reed (2016) surveyed 200 nonbehavior analysts and found that participants reported nontechnical substitutes of behavior-analytic terms as more socially acceptable than the technical counterparts. What does this mean? Speaking in nontechnical substitutes is likely to be more acceptable to your nonbehavioral colleagues. And, to be an effective interdisciplinary collaborator, it is in your best interest to be accepted by your colleagues.

So should BCBAs follow the advice of George Orwell and "[n]ever use a foreign phrase, a scientific word or a jargon word if you can think of an everyday English equivalent" (1946)? Of course, we are not recommending you deviate from the conceptual underpinnings of our science. One has to know the audience. But, you can rest assured the BACB will not revoke your certificate if you use "request" instead of

Table 6.1 Examples of Behavioral Statements Translated Into Nonbehavioral Statements	
Behavioral	Nonbehavioral
We have a behavior intervention plan based on an analysis of environmental maintaining variables that will place the maladaptive response on extinction and implement differential positive reinforcement for mands	We have a plan to help Craig learn to ask for what he wants instead of acting out to get it
The behavior technicians provide reinforcement on a VR-8 schedule	Dylan's teachers occasionally reward his good behavior
A most-to-least prompting procedure is used to teach adaptive daily living skills	We guide Hugo's hands to help him learn to use the bathroom and wash his hands afterward. We guide his hands less and less as he gets better at it
The differential reinforcement of other behavior procedure has not resulted in a decrease in inappropriate verbalizations	Abbie still says inappropriate things, even if we reward her for not doing so
The results of our functional analysis are inconclusive. It is possible his behavior is multiply controlled but we will need to conduct further isolated test-control analyses to confirm this	We need to continue looking at Vinny's behavior. As of now, it is not clear why he does what he does

"mand" when speaking with the grandparent of a young adult with autism. In fact, it is an ethical obligation of the BCBA to "use language that is fully understandable to the recipient" of behavior-analytic services while remaining conceptually systematic with the profession of behavior analysis (BACB Code 1.05b).

In Table 6.1, we provide some examples of behavior-analytic statements that are translated to more readily understandable statements. Note these translations are only one example. Your specific translations will need to account for the context, the audience and their culture, and other variables relevant to the client or professional you are communicating with. What is "fully understandable" for some may involve lay terms that seem to invoke mentalisms (see—Cooper, Heron, & Heward, 2007; pp. 689–708—for a comprehensive list of jargon BCBAs should think twice about using with nonbehavior-analytic audiences). If you are having trouble identifying alternatives to behavioral jargon, Critchfield (2017) describes a handy and straightforward resource for translating behavioral jargon.

NONBEHAVIORAL TREATMENT RECOMMENDATIONS

The BACB Code states that BCBAs "…uphold and advance the values, ethics, and principles of behavior analysis" (6.01a) and

"...review and appraise the effects of any treatments about which they are aware that might impact the goals of the behavior-change program" (2.09d). It is important that BCBAs understand the effects of treatments designed and implemented by their colleagues to prevent and discourage the application of harmful treatments. But what do we mean by harmful treatment?

A treatment may be harmful if it causes or puts one at risk for reduced physical, behavior, or psychological functioning compared to pretreatment levels. A treatment can also be harmful if it results in little to no gains and took time away from treatment that would have resulted in greater progress (Travers, 2017). This may occur because a known effective treatment was misapplied (e.g., the incorrect application of discrete trial instruction), or because a known ineffective treatment was applied (e.g., Facilitated Communication). Many harmful treatments have been promoted as effective for individuals with autism. We highly recommend you read Foxx and Mulick's book, *Controversial Therapies for Autism and Intellectual Disabilities*, so you can familiarize yourself with them (2016).

Over the years, some BCBAs have conflated *nonbehavioral treatment* with *ineffective* and/or *harmful treatment*. They are not synonymous. Just because a treatment is nonbehavioral does not make it ineffective or harmful (e.g., cholesterol-reducing medication). By conflating *nonbehavioral* with *ineffective/harmful*, we may reject or actively oppose a treatment that may help an individual with autism. For example, we may tell our colleague that their recommended way to manage a specific behavioral problem is not a good one, simply because we believe a behavioral treatment will automatically be more effective,[1] or because we believe our approach is better because it is ours.

Another misstep that may be more common than we would like to admit is conflating *nonbehavioral treatment* with *nonevidence-based treatment.* Not-so-long ago, few treatments for individuals with autism were supported by replicated research published in reputable peer-reviewed journals. However, the past 10 years have seen a rapid expansion of research from outside of behavior analysis, showing that

---

[1]This example may seem like a stretch, but we have heard this example quite a few times. Sometimes truth is stranger than fiction.

nonbehavioral treatments, too, can produce benefit for people with autism. Granted, at the time this book was written, no studies documented large-scale, long-term treatment effects from nonbehavioral treatment that are similar to the effects documented from Early Intensive Behavior Intervention (EIBI; NAC, 2015). Still, other treatments are gaining research support. For example, treatments that combine developmental and behavioral components are now supported by multiple studies, especially in the establishment of foundational play and social skills (Wagner, Wallace, & Rogers, 2014).

Automatically rejecting nonbehavioral treatment ideas can be counter-productive in helping clients meet their treatment goals. It is counter-productive because it can reduce trust and respect for the BCBA, erode a collaborative relationship, and decrease the motivation of others to work and cooperate with the BCBA (Brodhead, 2015). This may hurt a client's overall progress toward treatment goals because it can create conflict between the BCBA and other members of the interdisciplinary team. In turn, this impacts a BCBA's ethical obligations to act in the best interest of their client (BACB Guideline 2.0), uphold and maintain the standards of the profession (BACB Guideline 1.0), and maintain their ethical responsibility to get along with their colleagues (BACB Guideline 7.0). Rather than automatically rejecting *nonbehavioral treatments*, BCBAs should determine whether they have sufficient grounds to reject or offer an alternative to a proposed treatment.

When do you have "sufficient grounds" to reject a nonbehavioral treatment recommendation? Each situation is unique. BCBAs should weigh all available evidence for a nonbehavioral treatment along with the context it is recommended within—especially if the BCBA is not implementing the treatment directly. In Chapter 5, The Decision-Making Process of Evidence-Based Practice, we describe how a BCBA may do this as part of the process of evidence-based practice. In addition, we recommend the BCBA considers how questioning a colleague's recommendation may affect their perception and trust of your professional capabilities as well as the likelihood they will cooperate with your treatment recommendations in the future (see Brodhead, 2015; Newhouse-Oisten, Peck, Conway, & Frieder, 2017, for examples). In a lot of cases, nonbehavioral treatments can be quite effective. In other instances, even if minimal or no gains may result from that treatment, we still need to ask, "Considering the potential damage to trust and collaboration I need from other providers, is it worth it for me to question this treatment?" By holding off on questioning a recommendation that is not likely to be harmful, we can later interject when a colleague recommends something that is likely to be harmful.

ADDITIONAL RECOMMENDATIONS

As a final recommendation, we strongly encourage you to read Dale Carnegie's classic text, *How to Win Friends and Influence People*. In fact, read Carnegie's book if you are only going to read one book for the rest of your life (hopefully this is not the case, but we realize you may be quite busy). Why? First published in 1936 during the height of the Great Depression, Carnegie's recommendations have stood the test of time and have helped many professionals, including BCBAs. BCBAs who read Carnegie will likely feel comfortable with the many practical exercises aimed at how to manipulate the environment to create meaningful collaborative outcomes (Todd, 2014). Once you read Carnegie, read it again and again, and encourage your supervisees and behavioral colleagues to read it too.

CHAPTER SUMMARY

Treatment for individuals with autism increasingly involves interactions between professionals from a variety of healthcare disciplines. We believe that cooperation and effective collaboration of BCBAs with other professionals will improve treatment outcomes compared with treatment outcomes that would result from each discipline behaving independently. Collaborating effectively requires BCBAs recognize that each profession is a unique culture. Each member from other professions has been trained in, and may be governed by, views of appropriate treatment that differ from our own. In some instances, these professionals may have ethical or legal obligations to engage in behaviors that contradict BCBA ethical obligations. BCBAs should respect these cultural differences, communicate effectively, and respond collaboratively (not combatively) to nonbehavioral treatment recommendations. Such behavior will aide BCBAs seeking to maximize the benefits that can be gained from interdisciplinary collaboration.

QUESTIONS TO HELP YOU INCORPORATE THIS CHAPTER INTO YOUR PRACTICE

1. How often do you communicate with professionals from other disciplines/professions? Do these conversations always surround a particular client? Do these conversations ever involve genuine interest in the knowledge they have that you may not?
2. What training did you receive on interdisciplinary collaboration during your BCBA education and practicum supervision? How has that training helped you in your interactions with members from other disciplines/professions?
3. Think of a time when you had a difficult interaction with a member from another profession. What made the interaction difficult? How did that difficult interaction negatively impact your ability to suggest behavioral strategies after the interaction? If you could redo that first interaction again, what would you do differently?
4. Think of a time where you had a positive interaction with a member from another profession. What made the interaction great? How did that interaction positively impact your ability to suggest behavioral strategies after the interaction? If you could redo that first interaction, what would you do differently?
5. Do you know any BCBAs that work particularly well with professionals from other disciplines? What behaviors do they engage in that help those interactions? How can you incorporate those interactions into your practice more regularly?
6. What jargon do you commonly use that has people giving you blank stares? How do you alter your technical verbal behavior when talking to: a child with autism; a client's sibling; a client's parent; a teacher; the principal at a school; a physician; a Registered Behavior Technician (RBT); other BCBAs; a Board Certified Behavior Analyst-Doctoral; your billing administrator; the insurance agency funding a client's program; the neighbor who asks what you do for a living; when describing your dog's behavior to your nonbehavior analytic friend? *Note*: if your answer was the same to most or all of the above—you should ask a colleague for some help.

7. Communicating effectively to different audiences is a learned skill. What experiences have arisen naturally through your job that have helped you develop this skill? What CE opportunities have you sought to help with this skill? How often do you practice speaking to different audiences? How often do you seek feedback from different audiences on their understanding and acceptability of the verbal behavior you use?

CHAPTER 7

Common Errors and Mistakes Made During Ethical Analyses and Application

"Sometimes I write a little song / so you don't forget it / sometimes I write a little song / to remember the lyrics."

— *Jack Stratton, as sung by Antwaun Stanley*

Over the years, we have seen Board Certified Behavior Analysts (BCBAs) (including ourselves) make a number of errors and mistakes related to ethics and behavior analysis. For one reason or another, several mistakes have shown their ugly faces time and time again. Why does this happen? Well, it is likely the environment has not been arranged so that those errors and mistakes do not continue to occur. If the same errors and mistakes keep popping up, then clearly the lack of environmental support is pervasive enough to warrant someone's attention. So, we give them ours.

This final chapter addresses the four most common errors and mistakes we have observed. We realize we cannot change the world simply through our words (or can we—Catania, Matthews, & Shimoff, 1982). But, we feel passionate enough about this topic to at least try to make a difference. When you are working as a BCBA, humming the sweet songs of behavior-analytic treatment, we hope this chapter helps you remember the lyrics of wise and sound ethical judgment and analysis.

WRONGFUL APPEALS TO AUTHORITY

An *appeal to authority* occurs when the only evidence for a claim is that someone else agrees with you. The following examples are appeals to authority: "I heard Pete Behavior Analyst say at a conference that using the bathroom in a client's home is unethical because it develops a dual relationship"; "In Pete Behavior Analyst's blog post, he said it is unethical *not* to conduct a functional analysis"; "In his workshop, Pete Behavior Analyst said wearing a tank top while conducting behavioral therapy is unethical."

Practical Ethics for Effective Treatment of Autism Spectrum Disorder. DOI: https://doi.org/10.1016/B978-0-12-814098-7.00007-9

So what's the problem with the before mentioned statements? For starters, everyone needs to use the bathroom, functional analysis is not the only way to assess problem behavior, and tank tops are certainly appropriate if your behavioral intervention involves going to a pool or beach. Stated directly, the before mentioned statements fail to take into account the specific context in which one is making a decision. No rule meant to govern behavior can account for all situations. Caveats abound in all areas of science and claims about ethical behavior are not unique. Whenever "sage" ethical advice is offered or promoted, one should immediately ask: *How do you know this to be so* (see Chapter 1, Introduction to ABA, Ethics, and Core Ethical Principles)? Without objective evidence that the recommended course of action is best for your situation, such advice is exactly that—advice.

Not all references to authority are inappropriate, however. For example, the Behavior Analyst Certification Board (BACB) is an authority that you should reference and listen to. But unfortunately, we have witnessed multiple individuals disregard the BACB's advice. For example, we recently observed a complaint on social media[1] where an individual had called the BACB and requested clarification about a supervision requirement. The individual said she was not pleased with the BACB's answer, and was asking other people about what they believed to be the correct answer. Shocking, we know.

Though you are free to not be pleased with what the BACB says or does, we cannot think of any better advice than to follow the advice of the BACB. If you decide to disregard the advice of the BACB, you are on your own. As the social philosopher Chris Rock once said (and we paraphrase), *"You can drive your car with your feet, but that does not make it a good idea."* Do not say we did not warn you.

Scholarly articles, published in reputable journals, provide another example of when appeals to authority are appropriate. Each time a journal author uses a citation to support something he or she has written, that author is appealing to what other people (authority figures) have said. In many instances, the claims appealed through the use of a citation are supported by objective data. Therefore these nods, acknowledgments, hat tips, and references to authorities are usually

---

[1]You may be shocked to learn that we observed a complaint on social media. But we assure you, yes, it did happen.

appropriate (however, we are all human, and authors will misquote or misinterpret scholarly work).

So the question then becomes, when does one make a wrongful appeal to authority? A wrongful appeal to authority occurs when the "authority" does not have objective data about the specific situation you are concerned with. When it comes to ethics, not all advice is created equal. You certainly should consider the advice of professionals you interact with (assuming you maintain confidentiality and abide by all relevant laws). After all, we hope you benefit in some way from this book. But, unless the person you receive advice from is privy to the details of your situation, or is the BACB or your licensing body, that advice should not be followed blindly. If you do follow that advice blindly, you may end up wearing a sweater to the beach when you should have worn a tank top.

You should always be cautious when the "authority" used to justify a claim is not an authority on the facts relevant to *your* specific situation. At the end of the day, you will be held responsible for your actions. You should at least critically analyze the situation, determine what you think is appropriate based on the specifics of your context, and why that course of action is the most appropriate.

INCOMPLETE ANALYSES

The following question was once posed on social media[2]: "*Is it ethical for an Applied Behavior Analysis company to post pictures of their clients on that company's social media page, even if the family has signed a release form?*" People began to argue, and chaos ensued. One person, Christian, argued that if the client signed a release form that describes the nature in which a BCBA may use his or her photos, that BCBA may use those photos as long as the BCBA abides by the written agreement.

Dan disagreed. Dan argued that signing a release does not allow you to blatantly violate the BACB Code. Of course, asking a client to sign a release does not give you permission to violate the BACB Code. But, obtaining a release prior to sharing identifiable information, such

---

[2]"Ladies and gentlemen: the story you are about to hear is true. Only the names have been changed to protect the innocent." (Dunning, 1998).

as pictures, does bring one in compliance with the BACB Code. BACB Guideline 8.04b states that "behavior analysts do not disclose personally identifiable information concerning their clients... that they obtained during the course of their work, *unless written consent has been obtained*" (emphasis added).

The point here is that if you or someone you love (and anyone else) is concerned about a potential ethical violation, all Guidelines in the BACB Code should be reviewed before coming to a decision. At times, there may be multiple Guidelines relevant to the issue. Ideally, the Guidelines are synergistic (is this word still catchy?) and allow you to meet all ethical obligations. In other situations, different Guidelines may conflict with one another. If that is the case, you have another ethical dilemma on your hands.

MULTIPLE RELATIONSHIPS RUN AFOUL

A *multiple relationship* means you have more than one type of relationship with a client or their caregiver. One of those relationships is likely as the client's supervising BCBA. The second type of relationship might be as a babysitter, soccer coach, legal advocate, friend, or drummer in your Vulfpeck cover band. Having more than one type of relationship with a client or their caregiver necessarily changes your behavior as a supervising BCBA compared to if you did not have multiple relationships (see Chapter 2, Contextual Factors That Influence Ethical Decision-Making). This has led many professional organizations to establish explicit guidelines that reduce the probability that credentialed or licensed professionals they oversee will enter multiple relationships. For example, BACB Guideline 1.06d, states that "Behavior analysts do not accept any gifts from or give any gifts to clients because this constitutes a multiple relationship." By accepting a gift from a client, you may be altering the relationship you have with the client.

A benefit of such a direct and explicit statement is clarity. There is no room for interpretation. However, black-and-white guidelines "may place professionals at risk for undeserved sanctions and may potentially harm patients themselves by frightening the professionals into rigidity in therapeutic interactions" (Gutheil & Gabbard, 1998, p. 409). That is, BCBAs may be subject to disciplinary action for accepting a token of appreciation from a client. Consequently, BCBAs may become insensitive or unresponsive to other important contextual factors, such as cultural practices (see Chapter 5, The Decision-Making Process of Evidence-Based Practice).

But not all gifts are equal. Surely there is a difference between a handmade card from a client and an all-expense paid trip to Hawaii (if you have clients offering you the latter, please let us know and consider using us as case consultants). Some research suggests accepting and giving gifts leads to increased trust and helps establish positive rapport between a therapist and his or her clients (Knowx, Dubois, Smith, Hess, & Hill, 2009). For example, it would be considered rude and offensive to refuse food or drink (e.g., tea) when conducting a visit to the home for people from some cultures. And, a recent survey suggests that behavior analysts are concerned they will offend an existing client by refusing small tokens of appreciation (Witts, Brodhead, Adlington, & Barron, 2018).

On the flipside, multiple relationships can negatively impact trust and rapport between a BCBA and the client or caregiver with whom they have a multiple relationship. For example, the parent of one child was outraged that the BCBA, who had repeatedly accepted gifts from the client in the past, was now openly disagreeing with the parent about goals at the Individualized Education Program (IEP) meeting. In a conversation outside the IEP meeting, the parent asked why the BCBA had accepted all those gifts if they were not going to "have the back" of the parent in the meeting. From that point forward the BCBA had difficulty with parent cooperation and eventually needed to be replaced on the case to improve cooperation and the effectiveness of services that were being provided. In this situation, accepting gifts led to inappropriate expectations the BCBA would engage in behavior different than what would be expected from a supervising BCBA.

Multiple relationships clearly can be bad and avoided, if possible. But, a legitimate concern is how to draw a gray line. Too much rigidity can impede the overall effectiveness of an intervention. And, the same can happen with too loose of boundaries. It seems the best recommendation is to follow the BACB Code, including Guideline 1.06d. However, behaving ethically and in the best interest of a client is not as simple as checking "yes" or "no" that one followed a Guideline. One has to weigh the risks of developing a multiple relationship with other factors (e.g., Guideline 1.05 that references respect for client cultural practices).

DEATH BY POWERPOINT, OR MAKE YOUR FUNK THE P-FUNK

We have seen it a million times: a presentation or workshop on ethics that is nothing more than a speaker presenting Guideline after Guideline on a PowerPoint, saying "You need to follow these rules... or perish." Early in our careers, we also made this same mistake. But we stopped doing so, and so should you (and if you have not yet, do not ever start).

Why is this bad practice? For starters, it bores the hell out of your audience and students. Everyone in the audience likely has access to the BACB Code. They should be able to read the Guidelines on their own. If you have a crowd in front of you ready to listen to ethics, teach them something new, expand the dialogue, or have people think about familiar material in a novel way. Reiterating rules to govern BCBA behavior also leads to shallow, rigid, and incomplete ethical analyses (e.g., Catania, Mathews, & Shimoff, 1982). We call on all presenters and instructors to focus on teaching deep, flexible, and complete content that leads to a better understanding of ethics and behavior analysis.

In this book, we have tried to demonstrate engaging dialogue using novel behavior analytic approaches to *ethical analysis*. Ethics in behavior analysis does not need to be the same old boring content, conference after conference, week after week. Hopefully, by this point in the book you recognize that ethical analysis is more than just memorization of the BACB Code (if you have not recognized this, either this is the first chapter you are reading, or you may have to give the book another read).

Ethical analysis also involves understanding: you should be able to justify your ethical decisions (Chapter 1, Introduction to ABA, Ethics, and Core Ethical Principles); contextual factors that influence ethical decisions in unintended directions (Chapter 2, Contextual Factors that Influence Ethical Decision-Making); organizational systems that increase and maintain ethical behavior (Chapter 3, Creating Behavioral Systems to Support Ethical Behavior in Autism Treatment); what you are and are not capable of doing (Chapter 4, Identifying Your Scope of Competence in Autism Treatment); what your peers and colleagues know about the issue and that client values matter (Chapter 5, The Decision-Making Process of Evidence-Based

Practice); and how all of this fits with your interactions with other people (Chapter 6, Interdisciplinary Collaboration). Even these aspects are just part of a complete ethical analysis.

Complete ethical analysis may involve a complex series of behaviors. But, ethical analysis is behavior nonetheless. And, therefore, ethical analysis can be taught in an engaging and fun way. Funky, even.

CHAPTER SUMMARY

We leave you, the reader with a final thought. In this book, we have demonstrated that ethics and behavior analysis is more than just listing guidelines and saying "Follow these guidelines or perish in the great and fiery depths of behavioral banishment." We have woven overlooked and important topics with the BACB Code to continue moving dialogue about ethics and behavior analysis forward. We hope you join us to create the fabric of practical ethics for the effective treatment of autism spectrum disorder.

REFERENCES

Accelify Education Resources. (2016). The struggle continues for families seeking access to autism services. Retrieved from: <https://www.accelify.com/accelify-blog/2016/04/13/struggle_for_ autism_services/>.

Alexander, L., & Moore, M. (2016). Deontological ethics. In E. N. Zalta (Ed.), *The Stanford encyclopedia of philosophy*. Retrieved from: <https://plato.stanford.edu/cgi-bin/encyclopedia/ archinfo.cgi?entry = ethics-deontological>.

American Occupational Therapy Association (AOTA). (2015). Occupational therapy code of ethics (2015). Retrieved from: <https://www.aota.org/-/media/corporate/files/practice/ethics/code- of-ethics.pdf>.

American Psychological Association, Presidential Task Force on Evidence-Based Practice. (2006). Evidence-based practice in psychology. *American Psychologist*, *61*, 271−285.

American Speech-Language-Hearing Association (ASHA). (2016). Code of ethics. Retrieved from: <www.asha.org/policy>.

Association of American Educators (AAE). (2013). Code of ethics for educators. Retrieved from: <https://www.aaeteachers.org/index.php/about-us/aae-code-of-ethics>.

Athens, E. S., & Vollmer, T. R. (2010). An investigation of differential reinforcement of alterna- tive behavior without extinction. *Journal of Applied Behavior Analysis*, *43*, 569−589.

Atreja, A., Bellam, N., & Levy, S. R. (2005). Strategies to enhance patient adherence: Making it simple. *Medscape General Medicine*, *7*, 4.

Baer, D. M., Wolf, M. M., & Risley, T. R. (1968). Some current dimensions of applied behavior analysis. *Journal of Applied Behavior Analysis*, *1*, 91−97.

Bailey, J. S., & Burch, M. R. (2016). *Ethics for behavior analysts*. New York, NY: Routledge.

Bailey, J. T., & Mazur, J. E. (1990). Choice behavior in transition: Development of preference for the higher probability of reinforcement. *Journal of the Experimental Analysis of Behavior*, *53*, 409−422.

Baker, J. C., & LeBlanc, L. A. (2015). Aging. In F. K. McSweeney & E. S. Murphy (Eds.), *The Wiley Blackwell handbook of operant and classical conditioning* (pp. 695−714). Oxford, UK: John Wiley & Sons.

Baker, R. (2005). A draft model code of ethics for bioethicists. *The American Journal of Bioethics*, *5*, 33−41.

Baker, R. (2009). In defense of bioethics. *Journal of Law, Medicine, & Ethics*, *1*, 83−92.

Barbera, M. L. (2007). *The verbal behavior approach*. Philadelphia, PA: Jessica Kingsley Publishers.

Barrett, L. (2015). Why brains are not computers, why behaviorism is not Satanism, and why dol- phins are not aquatic apes. *The Behavior Analyst*, *39*, 9−23.

Beavers, G. A., Iwata, B. A., & Lerman, D. C. (2013). Thirty years of research on functional analysis of problem behavior. *Journal of Applied Behavior Analysis*, *46*, 1−21.

Becirevic, A., Critchfield, T. S., & Reed, D. D. (2016). On the social acceptability of behavior- analytic terms: Crowdsourced comparisons of lay and technical language. *The Behavior Analyst*, *39*, 305−317.

Behavior Analyst Certification Board. (2012). Fourth Edition Task List. Retrieved from: <https://www.bacb.com/wp-content/uploads/2017/09/160101-BCBA-BCaBA-task-list-fourth-edition-english.pdf>.

Behavior Analyst Certification Board. (2014). Professional and Ethical Compliance Code for Behavior Analysts. Retrieved from: <https://bacb.com/ethics-code/>.

Binder, C. (1996). Behavioral fluency: Evolution of a new paradigm. *The Behavior Analyst, 19*, 163−197.

Bondy, A. S., & Frost, L. A. (1994). The Picture Exchange Communication System. *Focus on Autism and Other Developmental Disabilities, 9*, 1−19.

Brodhead, M. T. (2015). Maintaining professional relationships in an interdisciplinary setting: Strategies for navigating non-behavioral treatment recommendations for individuals with autism. *Behavior Analysis in Practice, 8*, 70−78.

Brodhead, M. T., Durán, L., & Bloom, S. (2014). Cultural and linguistic diversity in recent verbal behavior research on individuals with disabilities: A review and implications for research and practice. *The Analysis of Verbal Behavior, 30*, 75−86.

Brodhead, M. T., & Higbee, T. S. (2012). Teaching and maintaining ethical behavior in a professional organization. *Behavior Analysis in Practice, 5*, 82−88.

Brodhead, M. T., Quigley, S. P., & Cox, D. J. (2018). How to identify ethical practices in organizations prior to employment. *Behavior Analysis in Practice, 11*, 165−173.

Bucklin, B. R., Alvero, A. M., Dickinson, A. M., Austin, J., & Jackson, A. K. (2000). Industrial-organizational psychology and organizational behavior management. *Journal of Organizational Behavior Management, 20*, 27−75.

Carnegie, D. (1937). How to win friends and influence people. Retrieved from: <http://images.kw.com/docs/2/1/2/212345/1285134779158_htwfaip.pdf>.

Carr, J. E., & Briggs, A. M. (2010). Strategies for making regular contact with the scholarly literature. *Behavior Analysis in Practice, 3*, 13−18.

Carr, J. E., Wilder, D. A., Majdalany, L., Mathisen, D., & Strain, L. A. (2013). An assessment-based solution to a human-service employee performance problem: An initial evaluation of the Performance Diagnostic Checklist−Human Services. *Behavior Analysis in Practice, 6*, 16−32.

Catania, A. C. (2013). *Learning* (5th ed.). Cambridge, MA: Cambridge Center for Behavioral Studies.

Catania, A. C., Matthews, B. A., & Shimoff, E. (1982). Instructed versus shaped human verbal behavior: Interactions with nonverbal responding. *Journal of the Experimental Analysis of Behavior, 38*, 233−348.

CDC. (2017). National Center for Health Statistics: Health insurance coverage. Retrieved from: <https://census.gov/library/publications/2017/demo/p60-260.html>.

Claridge, J. A., & Fabian, T. C. (2005). History and development of evidence-based medicine. *World Journal of Surgery, 29*, 547−553.

Cleek, M. A., & Leonard, S. L. (1998). Can corporate codes of ethics influence behavior? *Journal of Business Ethics, 17*, 619−630.

Cooper, J. O., Heron, T. E., & Heward, W. L. (2007). *Applied behavior analysis* (2nd ed.). Upper Saddle River, NJ: Pearson.

Cox, D. J. (2012). From interdisciplinary to integrated care of the child with autism: The essential role for a code of ethics. *Journal of Autism and Developmental Disabilities, 42*, 2729−2738.

Cox, D.J. (2013, May). Metaethics, behavior analysis, and the route to professionalization. *Paper presentation at the Association for Behavior Analysis International annual conference*, Minneapolis, MN.

Cox, D. J. (2018). Ethical considerations in interdisciplinary treatments. In R. D. Rieske (Ed.), *Handbook of interdisciplinary treatments for autism spectrum disorder.* New York, NY: Springer Publishing.

Critchfield, T. S. (2017). Visuwords®: A handy online tool for estimating what nonexperts may think when hearing behavior analysis jargon. *Behavior Analysis in Practice, 10,* 318–322.

Dallery, J., Glenn, I. M., & Raiff, B. R. (2007). An Internet-based abstinence reinforcement treatment for cigarette smoking. *Drug and Alcohol Dependence, 86,* 230–238.

DeSouza, A. A., Akers, J. S., & Fisher, W. W. (2017). Empirical application of Skinner's verbal behavior to interventions for children with autism: A review. *The Analysis of Verbal Behavior, 33,* 229–259.

Didden, R., Sigafoos, J., O'Reilly, M. F., Lancioni, G. E., & Sturmey, P. (2007). A multi-site cross-cultural replication of Upper's (1974) unsuccessful self-treatment of writer's block. *Journal of Applied Behavior Analysis, 40,* 773.

Djulbegovic, B., Hozo, I., & Ioannidis, J. P. A. (2015). Modern health care as a game theory problem. *European Journal of Clinical Investigation, 45,* 1–12.

Drotar, D. D., & Sturm, L. A. (1996). Interdisciplinary collaboration in the practice of mental retardation. In J. W. Jacobson & J. A. Mulick (Eds.), *Manual of diagnosis and professional practice in mental retardation* (pp. 393–401). Washington, DC: American Psychological Association.

Dufek, S., & Schreibman, L. (2014). Natural environment training. In J. Tarbox, D. R. Dixon, P. Sturmey, & J. L. Matson (Eds.), *Handbook of early intervention for autism spectrum disorders* (pp. 255–269). New York, NY: Springer.

Dunlap, G., de Perczel, M., Clarke, S., Wilson, D., Wright, S., White, R., & Gomez, A. (1994). Choice making to promote adaptive behavior for students with emotional and behavioral challenges. *Journal of Applied Behavior Analysis, 27,* 505–518.

Dunning, J. (1998). *On the air: The encyclopedia of old-time radio.* Oxford, UK: Oxford University Press.

Edelstein, L. (1996). *The hippocratic oath: Text, translation, and interpretation.* Baltimore, MD: The Johns Hopkins University Press.

Falender, C. A., & Shafranske, E. P. (2012). The importance of competency-based clinical supervision in the twenty-first century: Why bother? *Journal of Contemporary Psychotherapy, 42,* 129–137.

Farre, A., & Rapley, T. (2017). The new old (and old new) medical model: Four decades navigating the biomedical and psychosocial understandings of health and illness. *Healthcare, 5,* 88–96.

Fong, E. H., Catagnus, R. M., Brodhead, M. T., Quigley, S., & Field, S. (2016). Developing cultural awareness skills of behavior analysts. *Behavior Analysis in Practice, 9,* 84–94.

Foucault, M. (1990). *The history of sexuality. Volume I: An introduction.* New York, NY: Vintage.

Foxx, R. M., & Mulick, J. A. (2016). *Controversial therapies for autism and intellectual disabilities: Fad, fashion, and science in professional practice* (2nd ed.). New York, NY: Routledge.

Freedman, D. H. (2016). Improving public perception of behavior analysis. *The Behavior Analyst, 39,* 89–95.

Glenn, S. S. (1993). Windows on the 21st century. *The Behavior Analyst, 16,* 133–151.

Green, G., & Johnston, J. M. (2009). A primer on professional credentialing: Introduction to invited commentaries on licensing behavior analysts. *Behavior Analysis in Practice, 2,* 51–52.

Groves, E. A., & Austin, J. L. (2017). An evaluation of interdependent and independent group contingencies during the good behavior game. *Journal of Applied Behavior Analysis, 50,* 552–566.

Gutheil, T. G., & Gabbard, G. O. (1998). Misuses and misunderstandings of boundary theory in clinical and regulatory settings. *The American Journal of Psychiatry, 155,* 409–414.

Hammurabi., & Johns, C. H. W. (2008). *The code of Hammurabi.* London, UK: Seven Treasures Publications.

Hanley, G. P. (2012). Functional assessment of problem behavior: Dispelling myths, overcoming implementation obstacles, and developing new lore. *Behavior Analysis in Practice, 5,* 54−72.

Hanley, G. P., Piazza, C. C., Fisher, W. W., & Maglieri, K. A. (2005). On the effectiveness of and preference for punishment and extinction components of function-based interventions. *Journal of Applied Behavior Analysis, 38,* 51−65.

Harari, Y. N. (2015). *Sapiens: A brief history of humankind.* United States: Harper Collins Publishers.

Herrnstein, R. J., & Loveland, D. H. (1975). Maximizing and matching on concurrent ratio schedules. *Journal of the Experimental Analysis of Behavior, 24,* 107−116.

Van Houten, R., Axelrod, S., Bailey, J. S., Favell, J. E., Foxx, R. M., Iwata, B. A., & Lovaas, O. I. (1988). The right to effective behavioral treatment. *Journal of Applied Behavior Analysis, 21,* 381−384.

Hursh, S. R., & Silberberg, A. (2008). Economic demand and essential value. *Psychological Review, 115,* 186−198.

Hursthouse, R. (1999). *On virtue ethics.* Oxford, UK: Oxford University Press.

Hursthouse, R., & Pettigrove, G. (2016). Virtue ethics. In E. N. Zalta (Ed.), *The Stanford encyclopedia of philosophy.* Retrieved from: <https://plato.stanford.edu/entries/ethics-virtue/>.

Hyten, C., & Ludwig, T. D. (2017). Complacency in process safety: A behavior analysis toward prevention strategies. *Journal of Organizational Behavior Management, 37,* 240−260.

Interagency Autism Coordinating Committee (IACC). (2016). 2015 IACC summary of advances in autism spectrum disorder research. Retrieved from: <https://iacc.hhs.gov/publications/summary-of-advances/2015/>.

Iwata, B. A., Dorsey, M. F., Slifer, K. J., Bauman, K. E., & Richman, G. S. (1994). Toward a functional analysis of self-injury. *Journal of Applied Behavior Analysis, 27,* 197−209. (Reprinted from: *Analysis and Intervention in Developmental Disabilities, 2,* 3−20, 1982.)

Iwata, B. A., Pace, G. M., Kissel, R. C., Nau, P. A., & Farber, J. M. (1990). The self-injury trauma Scale: A method for quantifying surface tissue damage caused by self-injurious behavior. *Journal of Applied Behavior Analysis, 23,* 99−110.

Jarvis, B. P., & Dallery, J. (2017). Internet-based self-tailored deposit contracts to promote smoking reduction and abstinence. *Journal of Applied Behavior Analysis, 50,* 189−205.

Jessel, J., & Ingvarsson, E. T. (2016). Recent advances in applied research on DRO procedures. *Journal of Applied Behavior Analysis, 49,* 991−995.

Jonsen, A. R. (1998). *The birth of bioethics.* New York, NY: Oxford University Press.

Jonsen, A. R., Siegler, M., & Winslade, W. J. (2010). *Clinical ethics: A practical approach to ethical decisions in clinical medicine* (7th ed.). Columbus, OH: McGraw-Hill Education.

Kelly, A., & Tincani, M. (2013). Collaborative training and practice among applied behavior analysts who support individuals with autism spectrum disorder. *Education and Training in Autism and Developmental Disabilities, 48,* 120−131.

Knox, S., Dubois, R., Smith, J., Hess, S. A., & Hill, C. E. (2009). Clients' experiences giving gifts to therapists. *Psychotherapy: Theory, Research, Practice, Training, 46,* 350−361.

Lang, R., O'Reilly, M., Healy, O., Rispoli, M., Lydon, H., Streusand, W., ... Giesbers, S. (2012). Sensory integration therapy for autism spectrum disorders: A systematic review. *Research in Autism Spectrum Disorders, 6,* 1004−1018.

Leape, L. L. (2000). Institute of Medicine medical error figures are not exaggerated. *Journal of the American Medical Association, 284,* 95−97.

LeBlanc, L. A., Heinicke, M. R., & Baker, J. C. (2009). Expanding the consumer base for behavior-analytic services: Meeting the needs of consumers of the 21st century. *Behavior Analysis in Practice*, *5*, 4–14.

Lindsley, O. R. (1990). Precision teaching: By teachers for children. *Teaching Exceptional Children*, *22*, 10–15.

La Londe, K. B., Mahoney, A., Edwards, T. L., Cox, C., Weetjens, B., Durgin, A., & Poling, A. (2015). Training pouched rats to find people. *Journal of Applied Behavior Analysis*, *48*, 1–10.

Lovaas Institute. (2003). *Teaching individuals with developmental delays: Basic intervention techniques*. Austin, TX: Lovaas Institute.

Luiselli, J. K. (2015). In response: Maintaining professional relationships in an interdisciplinary setting: Strategies for navigating non-behavioral treatment recommendations for individuals with autism. *Behavior Analysis in Practice*, *8*, 79.

MacDonald, M. B., Bally, J. M., Ferguson, L. M., Murray, B. L., Fowler-Kerry, J., & Anonson, M. S. (2010). Knowledge of the professional role of others: A key interprofessional competency. *Nurse Education in Practice*, *10*, 238–242.

Makary, M. A., & Daniel, M. (2016). Medical error—the third leading cause of death in the US. *British Medical Journal*, *353*, i2139.

Malott, M. M. (2003). *Paradox of organizational change*. Reno, NV: Context Press.

Malott, R. M., & Garcia, M. E. (1987). A goal-directed model for the design of human performance systems. *Journal of Organizational Behavior Management*, *9*, 125–129.

Malott, R. M., & Shane, J. T. (2014). *Principles of behavior* (7th ed.). New York, NY: Routledge.

Malott, R. W. (1974). A behavioral systems approach to the design of human services. In D. Harshbarger & R. F. Maley (Eds.), *Behavior analysis and systems analysis: An integrative approach to mental health programs*. Kalamazoo, MI: Behaviordelia.

Marino, G. (2010). *Ethics: The essential writings*. New York, NY: Random House Publishing.

Mayer, C. E. (2009, November/December). The health claim game: Here's how to fight back when your insurance company denies a claim. *AARP The Magazine*. Retrieved from: <https://www.aarp.org/health/medicare-insurance/info-09-2009/health_claim_game.html>.

Mazur, J. E. (1987). An adjusting procedure for studying delayed reinforcement. In M. L. Commons, J. E. Mazur, J. A. Nevin, & H. Rachlin (Eds.), *Quantitative analyses of behavior: The effect of delay and of intervening events on reinforcement value* (Vol. 5, pp. 55–73). Hillsdale, NJ: Erlbaum.

McDowell, J. (1989). Two modern developments in matching theory. *The Behavior Analyst*, *12*, 153–166.

McGee, H. M., & Diener, L. H. (2010). Behavioral systems analysis in health and human services. *Behavior Modification*, *34*, 415–442.

McKerchar, T. L., & Renda, C. R. (2012). Delay and probability discounting in humans: An overview. *The Psychological Record*, *62*, 817–834.

Mitchell, S. H. (2017). Devaluation of outcomes due to their cost: Extending discounting models beyond delay. In J. Stevens (Ed.), *Impulsivity. Nebraska symposium on motivation* (pp. 145–161). Cham: Springer.

Molloy, G. N. (1983). The unsuccessful self-treatment of a case of "writer's block": A replication. *Perceptual and Motor Skills*, *57*, 566.

Muir, A. J., Sanders, L. L., Wilkinson, W. E., & Schmader, K. (2001). Reducing medication regimen complexity: A controlled trial. *Journal of General Internal Medicine*, *16*, 77–82.

National Autism Center. (2015). *Findings and conclusions: National Standards Project, Phase 2*. Randolph, MA: National Autism Center.

Newhouse-Oisten, M. K., Peck, K. M., Conway, A. A., & Frieder, J. E. (2017). Ethical considerations for interdisciplinary collaboration with prescribing professionals. *Behavior Analysis in Practice, 5,* 145–153.

Newman, B., Reinecke, D. R., & Kurtz, A. L. (1996). Why be moral: Humanist and behavioral perspectives. *The Behavior Analyst, 19,* 273–280.

Odum, A. L. (2011). Delay discounting: I'm a k, you're a k. *Journal of the Experimental Analysis of Behavior, 96,* 427–439.

Office of the Secretary. (1979). National Commission for the Protection of Human Subjects of Biomedical and Behavioral Research—The Belmont Report: Ethical principles and guidelines for the protection of human research. Retrieved from: <https://www.hhs.gov/ohrp/regulations-and-policy/belmont-report/index.html>.

Orwell, G. (1946). Politics and the English language. Retrieved from: <http://www.george-orwell.org/Politics_and_the_English_Language/0.html>.

Petersen, T.S., & Ryberg, J. (2016). Applied ethics. Oxford bibliographies. Retrieved from: <http://www.oxfordbibliographies.com/view/document/obo-9780195396577/obo-9780195396577-0006.xml>.

Peterson, S. M., Frieder, J. E., Smith, S. L., Quigley, S. P., & Van Norman, R. K. (2009). The effects of varying quality and duration of reinforcement on mands to work, mands for break, and problem behavior. *Education and Treatment of Children, 32,* 605–630.

Petry, N. M., Andrade, L. F., Barry, D., & Byrne, S. (2013). A randomized study of reinforcing ambulatory exercise in older adults. *Psychology and Aging, 28,* 1164–1173.

Podlesnik, C. A., Kelley, M. E., Jimenez-Gomez, C., & Bouton, M. E. (2017). Renewed behavior produced by context change and its implications for treatment maintenance: A review. *Journal of Applied Behavior Analysis, 50,* 675–697.

Price, R., Marsh, A. J., & Fisher, M. H. (2018). Teaching young adults with intellectual and developmental disabilities community-based navigation skills to take public transportation. *Behavior Analysis in Practice, 11,* 46–50.

Quigley, S. P., Peterson, S. M., Frieder, J. E., & Peck, K. M. (2017). A review of SAFMEDS: Evidence for procedures, outcomes and directions for future research. *The Behavior Analyst.* Retrieved from: <https://link.springer.com/article/10.1007/s40614-017-0087-8 >.

Quigley, S. P., & Weiss, M. J. (2017, Fall). Supporting employee professional development activities: An example from a mid-size human-service organization. *Autism Spectrum News,* 10.

Reichow, B., & Wolery, M. (2009). Comprehensive synthesis of early intensive behavioral interventions for young children with autism based on the UCLA young autism project model. *Journal of Autism and Developmental Disorders, 39,* 23–41.

Reyes, J. R., Vollmer, T. R., & Hall, A. (2011). The influence of presession factors in the assessment of deviant arousal. *Journal of Applied Behavior Analysis, 44,* 707–717.

Reyes, J. R., Vollmer, T. R., & Hall, A. (2017). Comparison of arousal and preference assessment outcomes for sex offenders with intellectual disabilities. *Journal of Applied Behavior Analysis, 50,* 27–37.

Rhodes, R., & Alfandre, D. (2007). A systematic approach to clinical moral reasoning. *Clinical Ethics, 2,* 66–70.

Rogers, S. E., Anthony, W. A., & Danley, K. S. (1989). The impact of interagency collaboration on system and client outcomes. *Rehabilitation Counseling Bulletin, 33,* 100–109.

Rummler, G. A. (2007). *Serious performance consulting according to Rummler.* San Francisco, CA: Pfeiffer.

Sacket, D. L., Rosenberg, W. M., Gray, J. A., Haynes, R. B., & Richardson, W. S. (1996). Evidence based medicine: What it is and what it isn't. *British Medical Journal, 312,* 71–72.

Scheffler, S. (2011). Introduction. In D. Parfit (Ed.), *On what matters* (pp. ix–xxxii). Oxford, UK: Oxford University Press.

Sellers, T. P., Valentino, A. L., & LeBlanc, L. A. (2016). Recommended practices for individual supervision of aspiring behavior analysts. *Behavior Analysis in Practice, 4,* 274–286.

Sethi, S. P., & Sama, L. M. (1998). Ethical behavior as a strategic choice by large corporations: The interactive effect of marketplace competition, industry structure and form resources. *Business Ethics Quarterly, 8,* 85–104.

Sigurdsson, S. O., & McGee, H. M. (2015). Organizational behavior management: Systems analysis. In H. Roane, J. Ringdahl, & T. Falcomata (Eds.), *Clinical and organizational applications of applied behavior analysis* (pp. 627–647). New York, NY: Elsevier.

Sims, J. (2010). A brief review of the Belmont Report. *Dimensions of Critical Care Nursing, 29,* 173–174.

Sinnott-Armstrong, W. (2015). Consequentialism. In E. N. Zalta (Ed.), *The Stanford encyclopedia of philosophy.* Retrieved from: <https://plato.stanford.edu/entries/consequentialism/>.

Skinner, B. F. (1938). *The behavior of organisms: An experimental analysis.* New York, NY: Appleton-Century.

Skinner, B. F. (1953). *Science and human behavior.* New York, NY: The Free Press.

Skinner, B. F. (1957). *Verbal behavior.* Acton, MA: Coply Publishing Group.

Slocum, T. A., & Butterfield, E. C. (1994). Bridging the schism between behavioral and cognitive analyses. *The Behavior Analyst, 17,* 59–73.

Slocum, T. A., Detrich, R., Wilczynski, S. M., Spencer, T. D., Lewis, T., & Wolfe, K. (2014). The evidence-based practice of applied behavior analysis. *The Behavior Analyst, 29,* 41–56.

Smith, J. M. (2016). Strategies to position behavior analysis as the contemporary science of what works in behavior change. *The Behavior Analyst, 39,* 75–87.

Smith, T. (2013). What is evidence-based behavior analysis? *The Behavior Analyst, 36,* 7–33.

Somers, M. J. (2001). Ethical codes of conduct and organizational context: A study of the relationship between codes of conduct, employee behavior, and organizational values. *Journal of Business Ethics, 30,* 185–195.

Spring, B. (2007). Evidence-based practice in clinical psychology: What it is, why it matters; what you need to know. *Journal of Clinical Psychology, 63,* 611–631.

St. Peter Pipkin, C., Vollmer, T. R., & Sloman, K. N. (2010). Effects of treatment integrity failures during differential reinforcement of alternative behavior: A translational model. *Journal of Applied Behavior Analysis, 43,* 47–70.

Straus, S. E., Glasziou, P., Richardson, W. S., & Haynes, R. B. (2011). *Evidence-based medicine: How to practice it and teach it.* New York, NY: Churchill Livingstone, Elsevier.

Thompson, C., Aitken, L., Doran, D., & Dowding, D. (2013). An agenda for clinical decision making and judgment in nursing research and education. *International Journal of Nursing Studies, 50,* 1720–1726.

Tiger, J. H., Hanley, G. P., & Bruzek, J. B. (2008). Functional communication training: A review and a practical guide. *Behavior Analysis in Practice, 1,* 16–23.

Todd, J. T. (2014). Some useful resources for students who are tempted to bring enlightenment to errant non-behaviorists. *Behavior Analysis in Practice, 7,* 143–144.

Travers, J. C. (2017). Evaluating claims to avoid pseudoscientific and unproven practices in special education. *Intervention in School and Clinic, 52,* 195–203.

Upper, D. (1974). The unsuccessful self-treatment of a case of "writer's block." *Journal of Applied Behavior Analysis, 7,* 497.

Veatch, R. M. (2016). *The basics of bioethics* (3rd ed.). New York, NY: Routledge.

Wacker, D. P., Harding, J. W., Morgan, T. A., Berg, W. K., Schieltz, K. M., Lee, J. F., & Padilla, Y. C. (2013). An evaluation of resurgence during functional communication training. *The Psychological Record, 63*, 3−20.

Wagner, A. L., Wallace, K. S., & Rogers, S. J. (2014). Developmental approaches to treatment of young children with autism spectrum disorder. In J. Tarbox, D. R. Dixon, P. Sturmey, & J. L. Matson (Eds.), *Handbook of early intervention for autism spectrum disorders* (pp. 393−427). New York, NY: Springer.

Walker, S. F., Joslyn, P. R., Vollmer, T. R., & Hall, A. (2014). Differential suppression of arousal by sex offenders with intellectual disabilities. *Journal of Applied Behavior Analysis, 47*, 639−644.

Weinberger, D. (2011). *Too big to know*. New York, NY: Basic Books.

Wilczynski, S. M. (2017). *A practical guide to finding treatments that work for people with autism*. Cambridge, MA: Elsevier.

Witts, B. N., Brodhead, M. T., Adlington, L. A., & Barron, D. (2018, February 1). Behavior analysts accept gifts during practice: So now what? *Behavior Analysis: Research and Practice*.

Wong, C., Odom, S. L., Hume, K., Cox, A. W., Fettig, A., Kucharczyk, S., & Schultz, T. R. (2013). *Evidence-based practices for children, youth, and young adults with autism spectrum disorder*. Chapel Hill, NC: The University of North Carolina, Frank Porter Graham Child Development Institute, Autism Evidence-Based Practice Review Group.

INDEX

Note: Page numbers followed by "*f*" and "*t*" refer to figures and tables, respectively.

CPI Antony Rowe
Eastbourne, UK
January 07, 2020